MILITARY MEDICINE AND COLD WAR

Writings by the author:

Promises Kept has been published and printed by

iUniverse Publishers, 2009 www.iuniverse.com

1663 Liberty Drive Bloomington, IN 47403

1-800-Authors (1-800-288-4677)

ISBN: 978-4401-6807-9 (pbk)

MILITARY MEDICINE AND COLD WAR

A FLIGHT SURGEON'S REFLECTIONS

Jerald Lee Watts, M.D. FS. USAFRes.

MILITARY MEDICINE AND COLD WAR
A FLIGHT SURGEON'S REFLECTIONS

iUniverse books may be ordered through booksellers or by contacting:

iUniverse
1663 Liberty Drive
Bloomington, IN 47403
www.iuniverse.com
1-800-Authors (1-800-288-4677)

Because of the dynamic nature of the Internet, any web addresses or links contained in this book may have changed since publication and may no longer be valid. The views expressed in this work are solely those of the author and do not necessarily reflect the views of the publisher, and the publisher hereby disclaims any responsibility for them.

Any people depicted in stock imagery provided by Thinkstock are models, and such images are being used for illustrative purposes only.
Certain stock imagery © Thinkstock.

ISBN: 978-1-4917-4409-3 (sc)
ISBN: 978-1-4917-4410-9 (e)

Library of Congress Control Number: 2014914257

Print information available on the last page.

iUniverse rev. date: 05/11/2015

CONTENTS

Dedication

To all those who serve or have served in the
United States Military.

LIST OF PHOTOGRAPHS

Cover:
Photograph: over NYC – McDonnell Voodoo, F-101B,
(98th Fighter Interceptor Squadron flying over New York City)
Reference: The Airlifter, Dover AFB Photo Lab 1962
(In the public domain)

School of Aerospace Medicine – Brooke Air Force Base
Ejection seat trainer – Brooke Air Force Base
Old Farm House (Ranch)
Lieutenant Bob
Aerodrome – Gate House – Leopoldville, Congo
Congolese Civilians Walking – Leopoldville, Congo
Congolese men carrying fire wood
Congolese women washing in the Congo River tributary
UN Airplanes with jet-fuel cans nearby
SAAB J-29 receiving maintenance
Antiaircraft guns unloaded from U.S. Globemaster
UN Helicopter on tarmac.
High Altitude Chamber Wright-Patterson AFB
Lake house – fire place-Dover, Delaware.
Flight Engineer – aboard C-124
Runway in sight, Globemaster approaching Guantanamo
On the runway – @ Leeward Point, Guantanamo Bay
Leeward Point – C-124 delivering munitions…
U.S. C-130 evacuating dependents from Guantanamo Bay,
Marine machine gun bunker – Guantanamo Bay
Guantanamo Bay, Cuba – "Then we saw it happen"

The author produced all photos in this manuscript except those noted in the captions.

The author's photographs have never been published and may not be reproduced in any manner without written permission of the author.

Note: No official USAF Accident Investigation photographs of the Guantanamo crash site are included in this manuscript.

ACKNOWLEDGEMENTS

Special thanks to Ellen Hunter Ulken, my dear companion, for her support and affection and to Paul Lentz, retired Air Force officer and friend, for his academic review and suggestions for this manuscript.

Thanks to those men and women who protect our country near and far and to those who made my limited military duty an experience long to be remembered.

Particular thanks to my long time friends Dr. Thomas Pre Ball (retired AF Major General) and his dear wife Paddy. It seems we grew up together.

Thanks to Dr. Herbert Block (retired AF Colonel), my hospital commander and sponsor to the American Academy of Orthopaedic Surgeons.

Of all military line officers the best was Col. Franklin Crane, commander of the 98th Fighter Interceptor Squadron, a gentleman and an American hero.

Thanks for the friendship of Col. Robert (Bob) Prochko and his lovely wife, Judy.

As one author said in his writings, "The names have been changed to protect the innocent and the guilty." * In this case name changes are to maintain privacy.

Any errors are mine and mine alone.
Any individuals named or identified are those for whom
I have great admiration, respect and or affection.

* My friend and teacher, the late Dr. William
Waters III in his book Before I Sleep.

PREFACE – MILITARY

There was a time in the past century when every able bodied American male, eighteen years of age or older was obliged to serve a compulsory two or more years in the United States military. An alternate volunteer service group known as the Peace Corps was as an option for those eligible, but not in the military. This program was initiated during the Kennedy Administration. During the Nixon Administration the national compulsory draft ended. The country was tired of the controversial Viet Nam War.

We now have a volunteer professional military representing only a small percentage of our population. Unfortunately we are again engaged in controversial conflicts. Good as the voluntary military is, this country has not called upon the major portion of its youth to assume any responsibility for the country's safety. We have left that responsibility to those volunteers, largely a group of patriotic individuals, both men and women, while the rest of us look on and go about our "business as usual."

Despite the anxieties of international tension of the early 1960s most of us went along life's way with our own agenda, often not aware of the great dangers that seemed so far from our immediate experience. As young members of the military we met every day life situations in the most personal manner, often not thinking of the greater picture.

It was not until the escalation of the Viet Nam War that we realized the true horrors of our generation. Such is the scope of this narrative, one doctor's personal experiences in the military during a period of the Cold War, the early days leading to the intensification of that Cold War to the Viet Nam Conflict. Recent twenty-first century international events suggest that the embers of that Cold War may still exist.

MILITARY MEDICINE AND COLD WAR

INTRODUCTION

AFTER GRADY

Early that summer morning slivers of golden sunlight peeked outside my window, high above the city I loved. I arose slowly from my bed, slapped cold water on my scratchy face, shaved, showered in steamy water, all the while thinking, this is my last day at Atlanta's Grady Hospital. I slipped on a fresh laundered set of worn and frayed, but starched hospital whites, put on my dried blood stained white hush puppies, picked up a cup of coffee at the dining room, and headed for the surgery ward.

At 7 a.m. on 1 July 1961 I handed the ward over to the new resident who would begin his first year of surgery residency. A year before I walked onto the same surgery ward after a year of internship and began my first year of real responsibility. The new guy would no longer be the boy intern, the lowest rung on the medical professional ladder, but would be in charge of the surgical care of the patients and direct the training of the new group of uninitiated young doctors.

I would end two years of cloistered confinement. Outside those hospital walls was a different world, a world that I had almost forgotten, except for the grief, sorrow, and disturbance that we daily received from it.

The call to active military duty began 6 July. I was scheduled to travel to San Antonio, Texas to The School of Aerospace Medicine or simply the flight surgeon school. We would be trained to extend our medical knowledge to the military's requirements. That involved our care of the flying personnel of the Air Force.

I was relieved as I walked out of the huge hospital onto busy Butler Street, glanced at the shuffling of patients as they were directed to our new hospital and heard the shrill siren of the ambulance that would for a while, not be my call to duty.

I gazed into a bright summer morning. At that moment I began a new phase of medicine. I was filled with anticipation for a new venture, a moment in another world.

SCHOOL OF AEROSPACE MEDICINE

The early 1960s were times of anxious international conflict. Post World War II pitted two major super powers, the United States and the Soviet Union against each other. China, a rising communist government, after the withdrawal of the colonial French from Indochina presented a threat to the stability of the Far East.

It was apparent to most Americans that the Soviet Union was out pacing the United States in the space program with the 1957 international coup, the sending of its satellite "Sputnik" into space orbiting the earth. America was in catch-up mode. As a nation we suffered the anxiety of falling behind in world technology and leadership. I was to feel that anxiety mixed with a twinge of excitement as I entered the School of Aerospace Medicine.

San Antonio was dreadfully hot from July until October 1961 when our class of over a hundred flight surgeons completed the intensive three months of aerospace medicine. The course included training in the recognition of and treatment of medical implications of flight. The greatest problem included high altitude physical problems, flying stress and how to manage those pilots, navigators and aircrew members who experienced such difficulties. Physicians were placed in the altitude chamber to learn first hand the symptoms and dynamics of altitude changes, anoxia and decompression sickness. The training courses produced near specialists in ear, nose, and throat medicine as well as visual and pulmonary physiology.

In one exercise, the physicians were placed in training ejection seats and were literally blown to the top of the "ejection hanger" to experience simulated ejections from inflight planes. "That was a kick in the butt," said my classmate, Epson, as he was unstrapped from his ejection seat. He was a New Yorker. A delightful guy, he had no understanding of military dress or regulations of conformity. He rarely wore the correct uniform combination, right shoes or socks. He had difficulty figuring out whom he saluted and who saluted him. "We are under cover when we have on our dress hats with plastic covers. An officer never carries an umbrella," the instructor advised. Once my classmate was stopped and forced to stand in the pouring rain by a senior field grade officer that caught him using a yellow and purple flower print umbrella.

The doctors of my Aerospace Medical class were nothing more than undisciplined rabble-rousers. As individuals, conformity was difficult. Under the blistering Texas sun the medical class of flight surgeon candidates was drilled by a master sergeant. One of the sweating docs stepped out of ranks, removed his cap, rubbed his sweating face with a handkerchief and arrogantly asked, "Why are we being drilled by a noncommissioned airman. Aren't an officer's two silver bars more than five or six stripes of an enlisted man? Shouldn't we be drilling him?" When the column of marching doctors heard the question, they broke ranks, scattered and wandered back to their prefab, gray, sweltering, wooden barracks.

The following day we were assembled by an angry, red faced, husky major who yelled at us at the top of his voice, "You guys be damn sure to remember a major's gold leaf is higher than a captain's two silver bars." He commanded our marching formations from that day on.

Because of the developing "space race" we were introduced to planned missions beyond our atmosphere and space travel and the potentials of space as a defense umbrella with future space marvels.

During one lecture a former German physiology scientist and early investigator of altitude effects on the human body, Dr. Hubertus Strughold, working with the American government, showed us plans for future rockets and lectured us on space effects of the human body.

He enticed us by quoting the prediction of President John Kennedy when he stated, "We will land a man on the moon within the next decade." It seemed incredible, yet we believed it was possible.

Upon graduation, we received our "wings" and were assigned to our distant bases.

* Dr. Hubertus Strughold (1898 - 1987), a German scientist during World War II served under the direction of the German Luftwaffe in controversial experiments using pressure chambers simulating altitude challenges to the human body. He served as director of our early aerospace medicine unit. His reputation has been diminished by later evidence from secret allied files identifying him as a participant in human experiments with Nazi concentrate camp prisoners.

School of Aerospace Medicine – 1961

Brook Air Force Base – San Antonio, Texas

Ejection Seat – Brook Air Force Base

"That was a kick in the butt."

BASE ASSIGNMENT

"Where in the hell is Dover, Delaware?" I asked. When I learned I would be assigned stateside, I sought a change in assignment to overseas, something different from the routine of the academic and hospital life that I had known for the last six years.

I wanted to get away from a schedule of twelve hours on and twelve off and thirty-six hours on and twelve off. In the flight surgeons school I had the first full weekends off that I had experienced in more than two years. It was hard to believe that any one had more than one night off at a time.

Adventure in new and far away places, that's what I needed. Stateside and Dover, Delaware didn't seem to measure up to my idea of adventure. I looked at a map and there it was on a little peninsula on the eastern seacoast away from everything exciting.

A letter arrived from a medical school mate, Dr. Pre Ball, telling me that I was assigned to his base and that he would be my immediate commander. I should not to attempt to obtain a reassignment. He wrote, "Dover is a Military Air Transport Service and Air Defense Command base. You will be working with those aircrews."

He further advised, "The base has an overseas flight mission and the air lift squadrons fly worldwide." He guaranteed a good assignment. "It will be an adventure and you will like it."

Dr. Ball was my intern when I was a senior medical student on the obstetrics rotation We shared many difficult and trying medical experiences. I knew he was a good doctor. I left well enough alone and trusted the advice of my friend.

My trip by auto took me through south Louisiana, the land of oil refineries and pulpwood, and paper plants. With no air conditioning in my car

I inhaled those choking, noxious, industrial vapors. Some called those odors money, but as early as the 1960s I could never accommodate to the detrimental environmental effects of those industries.

I arrived in New Orleans for a couple of nights. For the first time with military income I could afford a hotel on Royal Street. The French Quarter smelled the same, musty and foul in the morning as the street sweepers washed the dingy, odiferous streets from the night before. The odor of beer in the gutter was reminiscent of my college days in the city. I loved it and sniffed the atmosphere with a strange delight.

It was exciting to be back in the "Land of Dreams." My college roommate was stationed at the New Orleans Navy Induction Center. He and I lunched at Kolb's German Restaurant and after a hearty meal we drove out St. Charles Avenue to Tulane to visit our old school.

John was from a small town north of Jackson, Mississippi. After he experienced the bright lights and excitement of the big city of New Orleans, he stayed. He never left New Orleans until Hurricane Katrina drove him back to Mississippi for a few months. He was nationally respected in his area of medicine.

John, in his spiffy white Navy officer's uniform and I in my pressed Air Force blues ventured out to the campus to visit our professor of Physics, Dr. Karlem Riess. We knew he thought most of us would never amount to a "hill of beans."

"What do you guess he'll think of us when he sees us in uniform?" I asked John. "Well, we will show him." We were grown and responsible men. At least that's what we claimed.

Dr. Riess was commonly known as "Ducky" Riess. He waddled like a slew foot duck. He slowly stood from his swivel chair behind his paper cluttered desk and greeted us. "Come in boys," he enthusiastically said. He gingerly shook our hands as we entered his private sanctuary in the old red, stone physics building. After six years, at first glance he remembered our first names, out of his many hundreds of students.

Dr. Riess was unimpressed with his former students. After a brief conversation, he asked John what he was going to do with the rest of his life. John explained that he intended to pursue a dermatology residency at Tulane. "Ducky" turned to me and asked, "Just what are you going to do?"

9

I proudly answered, "I think that I will do a general surgery or orthopaedic residency."

"Why would you do that?" he retorted with a squirrelly grin.

I thought I could make some points with my old professor, even at this late date. "Well, Dr. Riess, you know orthopaedics has a lot of physics involved and I would like to put some of it to practice."

He stared over his half glasses that sat on the tip of his sharp, angled nose. He was a short lean fellow with a slight pouch about his waist and thinning, slick, straight, combed back, gray hair, and piercing blue eyes. "Hell, you never knew any physics," he said with a slight smile.

"Yes, sir, but only you know that," I answered.

I was put in my place. He was a tough professor and mentor to the premedical students. If a student could pass Ducky's physics course, that student could be accepted into most any medical school in the country. He was fair, even when it meant grave disappointment for the student. He was a brutal grader. He gave the grades we earned, no more and no less. He gave no easy passes and no benefits of the doubt. "You make a mistake in physics and a building collapses," he was fond of saying.

Those premeds who avoided or shied away from Dr. Riess' physics course were suspect. We loved him. He never married and lived with his spinster sister. His life was teaching and his pride was in the University and the accomplishments of his students. Unfortunately, as an elderly invalid, he died while being transferred by helicopter from his home after the wrath of Katrina, the hurricane that devastated New Orleans.

After New Orleans, I drove through Atlanta, passed under the ominous shadow of the New Grady Hospital where I spent so many days and sleepless nights. I picked up a classmate. He was headed to Boston to the Mass. General Hospital for his residency. We drove all night in the intermittent stormy rain to Washington. We arrived in the glowing but cloudy early morning sunrise at National Airport. He caught the shuttle flight to Boston. I didn't see him again for years. In Washington I rested a few hours before driving to my assigned base.

It's easy to get lost on the dark back roads of Maryland's eastern shore. I did and I worried, if I didn't sign in on time I would be considered AWOL (absent without leave), a serious military offense. All I needed was to start off on the wrong foot at my new base.

I arrived in the drenching rain, just before the midnight sign in deadline. At the hospital, the medical OD (officer of the day) sent me to the Base Administration Building. "You must sign in at the Administration Building," he said. "Then go and sign in at the BOQ (bachelor officers quarters) for the night. Report back here at 8 a.m."

I wondered, how do you get into this darn base? The doors to the administration building were locked shut. I climbed a few perilous limbs of a large tree in the bushes outside the building and taped on the windows with a long branch I had broken off. Amidst the lightning and thundering rain I finally, after several miserable minutes aroused the duty sergeant and officer of the day to open the locked doors.

The sleepy sergeant, rubbing his eyes, grudgingly opened the door. "Sir, come in. How did you get so wet?" he inquired.

"In the damn bushes," I answered.

I stayed in the BOQ in a double room. Each morning I awoke with a complete stranger in the other bunk next to mine. After a couple of dreary, intolerable weeks I spoke to the senior noncommissioned officer in my office about housing accommodations. I had learned that in the military the NCOs know everything. "Just ask your sergeant," my chief administration officer advised.

I asked the sergeant to step into my office. "Why am I seeing bachelor lieutenants living off base and I'm still in the BOQ? Isn't a captain's rank more than a lieutenant's?" I thought I knew something about rank, novice though I was.

"Yes, sir," I'll find out, said Sgt. Brewer. "Let me look into it."

I had asked the housing officer, a stuffy, ruddy faced major, why I was still in the BOQ. "Not enough slots authorized," he said. He explained that the Air Force had only a certain number of off base housing allowances to single officers and all the other single officers were already off base before I arrived. "Even if they are lieutenants, once they're off base, we can't ask them to move back into the BOQ," he proffered. "I'll keep you on the list for an available slot."

I was the only bachelor flight surgeon and the married officers had special family housing accommodations and special allowances.

The next day Sgt. Brewer burst into my office, unannounced. "You are authorized for off base housing as of today sir," he declared as he hid his partly chewed, but unlit cigar behind his back. His cigar, I was to learn, was his "Linus blanket" and it would appear whenever he was under stress or had just completed some complicated deal in the hospital. He was to become "my man" to get things done.

"Great!" I answered, "But how did that happen?"

"Doc., you know Major, and he named him, is on flying status but, since he's the administrative base housing commander, he only has to fly or be an air crew member four hours a month to get flying pay. We never see him for medical problems. He avoids us because of his fear of failing his flight physical and losing his flying status and pay, mostly his pay. I've heard he goes to the town doctors and pays out of his own pocket to avoid us."

"What does that have to do with it?" I naively asked.

"Doc, I pulled his medical chart. He has a waiver for high blood pressure and a weight problem to allow even the four hours of flying. When I called him to ask about your housing I reminded him that his annual flight physical exam was coming up and it looked like you would be his medical examiner," added my sergeant.

"So," I asked?

"Well," the Major said, "let me check."

My sergeant paused for a second and boastfully announced, "The Major called back this morning." He again took a deep breath and whispered "The major said, 'Why Sergeant, your doctor is lucky. An opening for off base housing has just occurred.'"

"I told the major that I was sure you would be mighty pleased with him and that good news," said Sgt. Brewer. My office NCO chief smiled that smirky, military smile, gave me a half salute, still with that cigar between his fingers and left the office.

The military works in strange and wonderful ways. I thought. I packed my bags and immediately moved out of the BOQ.

THE RANCH HOUSE

I loaded my car, evacuated the dismal BOQ and headed for the "Ranch House." It was an old gray, two-story, frame, farm house surrounded by vast fields of tall dry corn stalks, still standing in the late fall. It was reminiscent of a Charles Adams Halloween cartoon house often pictured in the New Yorker Magazine. A dirt road ran circuitously through the cornfields until it arrived at the front door and curved around the house into the rear gravel parking area.

A large porch extended from the front to the side. I imagined an old farmer and his wife sitting on that porch watching the sunset. Young, vigorous pilots and navigators, ever ready for a party currently inhabited the old house.

"You'll have Rafe's room upstairs," said the house chief, an older senior pilot who managed the house and the bills. Each of us contributed a sum for rent and utilities and a special party fund that often dried up. "It was that last party," the manager frequently said, "so we'll have to up the assessment."

"As long as two or more are gathered, there can be a party," he was fond of saying.

Rafe was TDY, that is away on temporary duty with an airlift squadron in Chatereaux, France, a huge Air Force Terminal for Western Europe and for airlifts through out the European, African and Middle East theaters of operation.

A few months later Rafe returned from TDY. An opening occurred when another crew member was sent to Europe and I temporarily remained in the house. The house became a game of musical rooms as residents departed or returned from overseas duties. It was a priority system of residency; those who had longevity on occupying rooms had options of returning or leaving. Having the rooms occupied by transient airmen kept the rent paid.

DOVER, NOT A BAD PLACE

In a short time I settled in into my new home, the Ranch House and began to feel like one of the crowd. We were a bunch of young bucks, anxious to live life to the fullest, yet doing a job that our country required,

After arriving in Dover I searched around the town, seeking entertainment and like minded individuals, accompanied by my new friends, pilots and navigators and a few fellow physicians. Though out of the hospital I was hardly aware of the other doctors, many of whom were married, more settled, or further along in their training than most of us in the flight surgeon's office, just out of limited medical or surgical training,

The Air Force preferred the flight surgeon candidates to be fresh and young, mostly with only an internship under their belts. With young doctors the military could mold us to fit their purpose more readily than someone with extensive specialty training. We were general practitioners to the flyers and could refer them to specialists when the need arose. We were their "go to guys."

Aside, from our daily work we collaborated on adventurous bachelorhood. We were surrounded by young, bright and attractive women, our own age and many as adventurous.

Our relations with the other young officers was like a big fraternity, all with the same purpose in duty and the urges for a good life. I soon recognized that little bit of insanity in the pilots and air crews that I saw in surgeons, a daring life style that accepted and pushed life to the limit. We all seemed to push life to the edge.

My service was to be an experience that taught me to respect those men and women as the core of our best society, those bright individuals who risked their lives on a daily basis to do a job and to protect the American dream.

UP STAIRS

On a late fall evening the doorbell rang. "Get the door somebody," a loud voice yelled from the rear of the Ranch House. I opened the heavy oak door and there stood two young, good looking girls, a blonde and brunette.

"Is this where the party is tonight?" the taller of the two softly asked.

"Why yes," I answered, stunned at the appearance of the two strangers.

"She's Rafe Higgs date," the other slender young girl said.

"Come in, yes come in ladies," I stuttered. Man, where did these two come from, I wondered?

"I don't have a date, I'm just with her," the second girl volunteered.

"Hey, you're welcome too," I mumbled, now embarrassed.

"Rafe's upstairs," I said. "Come in and I'll let him know you are here."

We entered the dim, unlit living room. The girls looked around. "Who lives here?"

"Just military guys," I shrugged. "Where did you'all come from?" I inquired.

"Wilmington," the taller blonde replied. "Rafe and Will Brown invited us down for the party. Is Will here?"

"Nope, he's out on a flight and won't be back for a couple of weeks. I'm sure he'll be sorry he wasn't here."

The younger brunette girl said, "Well, if Will's not here I'll just go into town and stay with my aunt."

"Oh, no. You stay. I don't have a date so would you be my date tonight?"

She glanced at her friend. "He looks okay," the companion responded.

It was a great party, delicious Greek food, prepared by one of the residents, and sparkling wines with music records blaring throughout the house. We had many bottles of wine, all brought back from France or the Azores. The guys in the house always filled their allotment of duty free alcohol on trips back into the states. We had a full, cool wine cellar.

About midnight the party thinned out. The records were replaying and the stack of 78 rpms often had to be restarted. Johnny Mathis' voice faded into the dark night. My date left and drove to her aunts' shortly after midnight. I stretched out on the lumpy couch before the iron grated, coal-burning fireplace and covered myself with an old, wool, military blanket. I dreamily dozed off.

In the hazy dark a gentle tap on the shoulder awakened me. In the shimmering shadows and soft glow of the diminishing fire I saw the tall, lovely blonde. She flipped her soft hair back and leaned down toward me and whispered, "Rafe passed out and the guys took him upstairs to bed. I don't have a ride to my friends and it is so late I don't have a way back to Wilmington."

I rubbed my eyes and peered up from my snug pillow, "Rafe what?" I asked.

"He's upstairs," she repeated. "Rafe's upstairs."

"Well, lets have another glass of wine and decide what to do," I foolishly suggested.

She straightened up and looked at me and probably thought, What is he talking about?

I had consumed enough wine. I shouldn't have considered more wine and certainly not driving this girl to her friend's aunt or to Wilmington. I sat up and tried to converse with her in a sensible manner.

We talked for a long while. In the dim, glow of the fire I realized that this girl was really someone special, long blonde hair, lovely features, bright hazel eyes, tall and slender. She spoke with a soft New England accent and seemed remarkably intelligent. "You can just stay here if that's okay?" I said.

"There's an extra couch and I'll get you some pajamas and blankets. You can change in the back hall bath. You can stay by the fire. You know I really shouldn't drive."

"Yes," she agreed, nodding, "You really shouldn't."

I covered her with a fresh sheet and a warm blanket. I fluffed a pillow from an occupied down stairs bed room and stoked the fire. I wished her a good night. "You'll be fine here."

The fire died. Only tiny embers sparkled with little popping, snapping sounds, and in the dark a soft voice whispered, "It's so cold in this house. Is there anywhere else we could rest?"

"Upstairs," I answered.

We crept, barefoot across the room in the haze of the flickering fire to the squeaky, wooden stairs and ascended, holding the worn, hand rail to the second floor.

"This is where the main bed rooms are. You can sleep in my bed and I'll find another." I opened my bedroom door and there in the dark, barely visible was Rafe sprawled out, clad only in his shorts, snoring in my bed.

"Oops," I thought of Goldilocks and The Three Bears. "We'll have to check Rafe's room. I think they just put him in the wrong bed."

We opened the creaking door and found an empty bed. "Will this do?"

"For both of us?" she cautiously replied.

"I don't mind if you don't," I said.

"Will I be safe?" she quietly asked.

"Safe as you want to be." I replied.

We pulled down the covers and slipped in. "Night, night," my Goldilocks whispered.

The Ranch House was like many rural homes,
surrounded by corn fields.

FIRST FLIGHT – TDY

After a couple of weeks at my base in the late fall of 1961 I was scheduled for my first trip over seas with one of our squadrons. My master sergeant would accompany me. "Sir, the colonel says for me to go with you to show you the ropes," volunteered my sergeant. "You can learn what is expected of the flight surgeon and the duties out on the flight line."

Those expectations included mingling and getting to know the crews of my assigned squadron, visiting the bases where they would land or be temporarily stationed. My job was to be sure our crews were properly accommodated at the bases and medical care was available at isolated locations.

"Sir, our orders are to accompany one of our squadron flights to Sweden to pick up military vehicles for the UN in the Congo," advised my sergeant. Our plane would also pick up and fly the Deputy Air Marshall of Sweden to the former Belgian Congo to assume command of the Swedish Air Force contingent of the UN forces.

Our cross Atlantic flight was uneventful until we neared the airfield outside Stockholm. Our altimeters misread the actual altitude. The instruments were not properly adjusted for the Swedish terrain. There were high mountains nearby and we had no idea what our real altitude and position was in relation to those mountains. Near panic gripped the cockpit crew when the pilot and navigators realized our predicament.

"What do you mean, you don't know where the mountains are?" our aircraft commander, Major McCarey, yelled over the drone of the engines at the navigators.

The copilot contacted the Swedish ground controller for help. Meanwhile we flew in a tight circle, round and around in and above the night fog and clouds until we could get our bearings.

I never understood the problem except it was related to some "millibars" or conversion of our instruments to accommodate the surrounding terrain.

Once we landed all was forgotten. The King's Guard, a group of Swedish military officers, all young sub-lieutenants royally entertained our group of young airmen. They took us out on the town and provided lovely companions for us. Marriage rings disappeared from a couple of the airmen. I, a bachelor had no problem.

My orders were to stay until our full number of planes returned, but one of the flight engineers complained of severe headaches and developed an acute sinus problem that would normally ground him and delay the first flight out. "What can you do for him, Doc?" the commander asked.

"I can medicate him and watch him and fly out with the crew." I answered. "With these medications usually drowsiness occurs," I advised the commander. "I can manage that by closely watching the engineer on the flight. I can nurse him back."

We had only to fly from Stockholm to England along the Baltic and North Sea. The commander felt that a single engineer could handle that distance and that we could use our patient only briefly at the flight engineer's control panel.

Our biggest concern was navigating along the East German shore on the Baltic Sea. One of our reconnaissance B-47 bombers penetrated the East German territory a few weeks before and was shot down by the Russian or East German antiaircraft with a loss of the two man crew. Our government claimed the plane had just veered off course and made an international protest to the East German government.

The commander quietly commented, "It was a trial penetration against the East German radar and the B-47 just got too far in and lost the gamble." Our concern therefore was not to drift into that territory. Two navigators operated the radar and checked each other's calculations.

"This is the coast line," the navigator pointed out on the luminous radar scope. "We need to stay outside this line." He ran his finger along the screen indicating the safe international waters. As we watched the coastline on our radar we slowly and safely passed the East German coast. The crew gave a big cheer of relief when we were safely by.

We landed in Mildenhall, England. There we took the engineer to the flight surgeon's office and continued his treatment. He was admitted to the hospital for further management. At Mildenhall another flight engineer was substituted for the flight to continue to the former Belgian Congo. My sergeant and I jumped ship, boarded another airplane from our Wing and returned to our home base. I later flew to the Congo on two temporary duty missions.

The Soviets and the communist East German governments were ratcheting up international tension between the Allies of the West and the Eastern Block. The Cold War was warming up as potential conflicts gradually and subtly intensified over the safety of West Berlin. Despite the increase of tension our young crews were going about our jobs as normal and as usual, rarely letting the political atmosphere interfere with our private lives. We were young and likely never realized the personal danger involved in some of our missions. The young always feel invincible.

Weeks later the commander of the squadron called me to his office. He spoke about the decision to medicate his engineer and to accompany the flight back to England, 'though my orders were to remain until the last flight returned. "Doc, you're new to the Air Force." He paused for a moment and put his cigarette into the ashtray on his desk, ground it into the butt filled dish. He leaned forward. "We were watching how you handled that problem. Though you violated your specific orders, you put the needs of our squadron first and we are glad to have you as our flight surgeon."

I was pleased that they had accepted me.

OUR PAY

We were at about eight thousand feet, an altitude that didn't require oxygen. At ten thousand feet the crews on the unpressurized planes must be on oxygen, the pilots, navigators and engineers at their stations. Any crew member moving about the cabin or in the cargo compartment must be on a "walk around oxygen bottle" and mask to move about safely and avoid altitude anoxia.

I sat by the navigator table watching my new friend plot our course over the Atlantic. "We're about here heading west," he said and pointed to a spot on the map about six hundred miles from the English coast. Once our location was established he could relax for a while until the next fix was needed.

One of the flight engineers eased over from the on board stove/heater. "Doc, would you like some coffee. It's a fresh pot."

"I believe so," I answered. He offered the other crew members coffee and we sat quietly as the plane droned on.

The senior navigator, a first lieutenant settled down nearby, sipping his coffee. We spoke for a few minutes and he commented, "You know I've always wondered why the doctors come into the Air Force as captains and the rest of us have to work up from lowly second lieutenants."

How do I answer that? I thought. "Well, how long have you been in the Air Force. How old are you?"

"Almost seven years and I'm about the same age as you," he said. "You know, it takes about seven or eight years for us to make captain,"

"You mean active duty after your commission?"

"Yeah," he said, "about that long."

"Well, I'll just tell you, Bob. After college we spend four years in med school then one or two years as interns or residents. Some spend more if they are coming in as specialists. That time is not paid for by the government. We pay our own way. Most of the internships don't pay much. You guys get paid officer's wages all during your six or seven years. Maybe that's the difference."

"I still don't get it," he mused. "You flight surgeons get flying pay as well as medical professional pay, and hazard or combat duty pay in some areas," he muttered. "That's more than most pilots and navigators of the same rank make."

"True, ours is a good deal. When we come into the Air Force we're ready to do our jobs. For flight surgeons the military has only three months to train us for our specialized duties."

"Yeah, maybe you're right," he said. He probably still doubted my explanation. I'm not sure he was ever satisfied until a few months later he was promoted to captain when he added his second silver bar to his single one.

"Now explain to me again why doctors come into the military as captains."

SWEDEN TO CONGO

The purpose of the first trip to Stockholm was to learn the flying procedures and what was expected of the flight surgeons "out on the line," as we called it. My second trip to Stockholm was a working trip. It was part of the Air Force "Operation New Tape." The orders again were to pick up military armored vehicles and equipment and ferry them to the former Belgian Congo.

We had none of the altimeter confusion that we experienced on our first flight into Stockholm. We landed without difficulty. We had a few days in the city and were again entertained by the young officers who were to participate in the Congo enterprise for the UN.

During the last hundred years Sweden has prided it self on its neutrality in world politics and war. In the seventeenth and eighteenth centuries it was a powerful military influence in European affairs. During World War II Sweden maintained official neutrality, yet continued its trade with Germany. Especially critical were its shipments of iron ore and coal to Germany for the manufacture of arms and steel products for tanks, cannons, and other military equipment used against the Allies.

Despite Sweden's neutrality their neighbor, Norway has always claimed that Sweden let the Germans into their country during World War II. Sweden, however was a haven for both German and Allied warplanes that were damaged and unable to return to their home bases during the war. Those planes landed safely on Swedish soil and the flight crews were interred in comfortable prison or detention camps for the duration of the war. The neutral Swedes treated both German and Allied "prisoners" hospitably. They medically cared for the injured and wounded crews of the flights. Some of our pilots were accused of flying undamaged planes, after bombing air raids over Germany to Sweden to escape further combat. After the war the accusations were thoroughly investigated by our military. There was no provable evidence of such occurrences.

In the mid-twentieth century this spirit of neutrality pervaded the liberal men and women of the city of Stockholm. While being entertained by the King's Guards we visited the night spots of the city. When the local girls learned that the Swedish officers and the visiting Americans were going to the Congo under UN military authority they accused us all of going "down there to kill the Congolese people."

They refused to dance with our airmen and the young Swedish officers because of the "mission of war." Nothing could be further from the truth. Though our mission was to deliver arms and supplies we had no desire to become combatants in the UN mission. We were authorized to defend ourselves, but not to seek offensive action. Attempting to convince the young ladies of our benign designs was to no avail.

Several of our young officers, however become friends with the local girls. Some communicated by letter for months after our brief stay. Most of us never returned.

While we visited a Swedish army officer and his family at his modest home, he received a "call up" for his reserve military duty. Sweden was conducting defense exercises along the Finnish border. Even neutral Sweden was suspicious during the early phases of the Cold War about the intentions of the Soviets. Russia had invaded Sweden's neighbor, Finland at the beginning of the Second World War. "Ve don't trust the Russian Bear," he confided to me.

Our trip in the old Globemaster took us from the States to Harman Air Base in Newfoundland, to the Azores in the mid Atlantic for refueling and crew rest then on to Mildenhall, England. We continued to Stockholm to pickup armored UN vehicles destined for the Congo.

The far, right wing French nationalists did not want the UN to end European colonial possessions in Africa or impose a settlement in Congo. The French resisted UN declarations to protect the central government of the former Belgian Congo. We therefore were not allowed to fly over French territory in our Congo missions.

We retraced our flight to Mildenhall, England then flew west and south over the Atlantic Ocean skirting France and Spain and entered the Mediterranean by the Straits of Gibraltar, en route to Wheelus Air Base in Tripoli, Libya. We crew-rested and then preceded to Kano, Nigeria for refueling and on to Leopoldville (now called Kinshasa) in Congo.

At the American Embassy in Leopoldville my corpsman and I held clinics for the diplomatic dependents and performed the annual physical exams on the embassy staff that were necessary for them to continue in their foreign assignments. We reviewed staff medical records and got them all up to date on their shots and immunizations. We stayed in town with members of the embassy when it was deemed unsafe to travel back to the airfield at night.

One night when an embassy party lasted so late the staff advised me to stay in town. A young bachelor volunteered that I should stay with him in his compound. That offer sounded good to me, but after a few more drinks he presented me with flaming red silk pajamas. That night I locked my bed room door.

One of my acquaintances, an Army colonel attaché was in-fact a CIA (Counter Intelligence Agency) agent. Months after I returned to the States I learned that he was murdered at his compound by an unknown assassin. As far as I know the assassin was never identified. At least, I never knew.

My corpsmen, an African American buck sergeant, opened many local doors to me in the city of Leopoldville. "Just come with me and I'll show you the town, Doc," he volunteered. By military regulations, officers were not allowed to fraternize with enlisted men, but he was "my man."

One day we drove from the air field and ventured downtown to find cooler shoes to replace my hot leather military shoes. The locals, during the uprisings and the early part of the civil war raided and burned most of the downtown stores. They ransacked many of the large homes of the frantic, departing Belgian civilians, taking over the houses and supplanting them with multiple families. Since most of the electric power was out they burned the fine furniture in the yards for cooking fire wood. Many of the homes were damaged both by military fire and looting.

Though the local Congolese natives took over the surviving down town stores they had little to sell after the riots and mayhem. We found what we thought was a functioning shoe store with many shoes neatly displayed in the windows. We bargained with the new proprietors for shoes. "Yes, we have shoes, but only left shoes," one sales clerk reported. Those were the shoes in the display windows. All the stock was lost to the stragglers and looting mobs. Maybe one size and one larger size of the same left shoe might work we considered, so we searched the remaining boxes. However, in the back of the store we stumbled upon one pair of matched white canvas tennis shoes, but they were so narrow I had to split the sides for air and to widen the shoes to fit my feet. Even split canvas shoes were better than the hot military boots or shoes.

Our corpsman had a special talent which he extended to the local black market. That was a money exchange business. Since American dollars or greenbacks were prohibited for local businesses he and a couple of his buddies were able to take our American money into town and through his connections trade it for over ten times the going exchange rate of the Congolese francs. We never knew what his cut was and we never asked. He didn't advertise his side business, but the troops knew where to find him.

In the medical section we had a different relationship with our enlisted men. It was more casual as most of the docs were barely military. At night he and I slipped into town in one of the white UN Jeep trucks to the dance clubs and bars where we enjoyed dancing with the locals to the rhythmic drums of the Congo bands. I had never experienced such rhythm and became an ardent fan of native African music.

My corpsman once remarked, "Sir, bet you can't dance like this in your segregated South." He was right. A white southerner in 1962 was learning a new social order could exist. That corpsman was one of the few that I wanted to recommend a commendation medal for his work.

As far as I could tell, the locals were receptive to the UN forces. I felt they understood that we were there to help quell the violence and assist in resisting the vicious rebel and European mercenary forces of the

Katanga Province. Unfortunately death and political terror continues to exist through out Africa.

On one trip into town I stopped to photograph local women down by the river washing laundry. They began to yell and wave their hands when they spied us. My corpsman eased up beside me and whispered, "If you take their pictures, they think you are capturing their souls." I quickly waved a friendly gesture to the women, pocketed my camera and we slipped away in our Jeep.

We received vague reports that a number of the American troops were injured in Elisabethville (now called Lumbashi). We sent a UN plane with a corpsman and several airmen to get them out of a local Italian run UN field hospital. When they arrived, the airmen found our men dehydrated and lying on blanket covered dirt floors, inadequately treated. A couple of the airmen had serious head and chest injuries. Our corpsmen diplomatically thanked the Italians for their alleged care and quickly flew the injured men back to Leopoldville. We were grateful they were as well as they were, that they survived.

Besides other injuries one of the patients had a few of his front teeth broken with facial fractures. I attempted to become a dentist. Our field dental equipment had an old-fashioned foot-operated drill. I tried to replace the front teeth using the available dental supplies without success. They kept falling out, so I asked my corpsman, "You try to fix them and I will do the foot peddling." Neither of us succeeded.

We patched up the men as best we could and shipped them off with a corpsman on a European flight to our Air Base in Wiesbaden, Germany. The chief of neurosurgery, Dr. Dale Richardson trained at Grady Hospital. My corpsman and I put tags on the men directing them to be seen and specifically examined by Dr. Richardson. We had no follow-up.

The duty hours were not routine. We sat at dinner one evening laughing and joking in a thatched and tin roofed hut near the airfield when a UN officer approached the table. He was pale and gulping a shallow cough as he anxiously informed his fellow officers of recent news. "We just got a report of activity along the river (the Congo). It seems that a small Italian squad of about ten men was attacked last night after dark by the rebels and slaughtered." He took a deep breath and blurted out, "and by God they ate them." Stillness and a muffled silence filled the room. We all held our breath for a moment.

"Not so," grunted one officer, "I don't believe that could happen. I don't believe that for a damn minute."

"That's the report we got. No survivors," the other officer admonished. It was bad enough to lose one's life, but it was beyond comprehension that cannibalism was involved. Just the thought terrorized our senses. The following day I shuttled out to the bush and never learned if the rumor was true or not. I did not sleep well for several nights.

I found time to visit the UN Hospital in Leopoldville and the Belgian Catholic Lovanium University, a medical school that continued turning out doctors for the Congolese despite the ongoing civil war. My corpsman and I visited the wards and operating rooms in both hospitals and were impressed with the services they were able to perform. These guys are right well trained, I thought.

One of the Belgian instructors commented in broken English, "When the young native doctors return to their villages, they have to make peace with the local medicine man, the witch doctor." He added, "Without the approval of the local medicine man they cannot practice scientific medicine. If they have a serious illness to treat, the young doctor can always call in his friend, the local witch doctor and together treat the patient. We call it shaking, rattling and penicillin." It was better than malpractice insurance.

While in Elisabethville in Katanga Province, my corpsman and I visited a Presbyterian mission hospital. Under an open, rusty, tin, roof shed that the missionaries scrubbed clean, I assisted operating on one of the missionaries who had broken his leg. I hoped to help longer at the hospital but was sent out to continue our shuttle missions in Congo. "We need all the help we can get. Try to come back if possible," a missionary pleaded as we left their village.

After we delivered the heavy armored vehicles to Leopoldville we delivered antiaircraft guns and ammunition and hundreds of barrels containing

JP-4 aircraft fuel to Elisabethville and Albertville. The Congolese national troops, Armee Nationale du Congo or ANC, were deathly afraid of any aircraft attack and would not fight. "They run off into the bush unless the antiaircraft guns are in place," said one of the airmen. "I'm not sure the guns ever hit any thing. They simply make a hell of a lot of noise."

A typical air attack was a small unidentified, unmarked, plane flying over and pushing a couple of bombs out the plane's door (a few were reported as old French fighter bombers) then scurrying away before any UN response was possible.

Our shuttles included flights between Leopoldville, Elisabethville and Albertville (now Kalemie) bordering Lake Tanganyika. Temporary accommodations were provided at each location where we could eat and crew rest. The UN forces, the Free Irish, the Pakistanis and the Nigerians, provided security. We were acting as noncombatants to avoid any international suspicions of American colonialism. We wore no official military uniforms while on the ground, away from the air fields in Congo. The other forces wore their own national uniforms with the UN blue berets or blue helmets.

It was a typical scorching, humid, day in Albertville when I strolled out to one of our airplanes on the flight line to retrieve some medical gear and supplies. The Nigerian guard and I chatted for a while. He was a tall, dark skinned native who spoke with the most beautiful native British accent. It was a pleasure just to listen to his rhythmic, almost staccato speech. I noticed he kept starring at my head and I hoped that his native tribe was not one of those headhunter tribes I heard about. Gradually I relaxed as he reached over and placed his huge hand on my head and ran his long slender fingers through my hair, and admiringly commented, "You Americans have the softest hair." He also admired my shirt. We became immediate friends when, right there I removed my bright colored civilian shirt, folded it and handed it to him as a gift.

Our squadron completed its numerous shuttles and we returned to Leopoldville. Shortly thereafter we headed home. Because of the intense heat and humidity in Congo, we waited until late night when the temperature dropped. With the drop in temp and perhaps humidity, it was easier to take off. I guess it was a lift problem. I was told Leopoldville had the longest runway in Africa, but I never knew for sure. At night it seemed that it took the whole runway to get airborne. We ended our mission and our planes returned north by the same route, again bypassing France.

N'Djili Aerodrome – Leopoldville, Congo 1962

UN Gate guard station

Leopoldville, Congo – 1962-1963

Civilian Congolese walking along dusty road.

Cogolese men are carrying fire wood along a
road outside the Catholic University.

Congolese women were washing laundry in the Congo River tributary.

UN Airplanes with jet-fuel cans nearby – 1962

These UN planes were flown by Swedish pilots in Congo.

SAAB J-29 receiving maintenance before take off.

These SAABs flew our air protection extending to Katanga Province.

UN troops are unloading German manufactured antiaircraft guns to protect the airfield against occasional Katanga Rebel attacks.

UN Helicopter on the Tarmac - Leopoldville

WHAT ME THE PSYCHIATRIST?

Toward the end of the first year of military assignment I was called to the hospital commander's office. "Go right in," the husky senior master sergeant announced.

"Yes, sir," I said to Colonel Block, "you wanted to see me?"

"Have a seat," he said. The medical staff was not much on military formality. Col. Block was Regular Air Force, but casual with the other medical staff doctors. He insisted that the flying personnel call them doctor and not by rank. He said this prevented the senior field grade officers from attempting to intimidate the lower ranking doctors.

"You are here as physicians first, then military officers second," he said. Most of us were two-or three year military draftees or volunteers and not career officers, though we had seven years of active or inactive reserve duty required by law. Regular Air Force career doctors were much more disciplined in military decorum. We were barely military and rarely very disciplined. Most of us were either recently out of extensive civilian medical training programs or had just finished internships.

He began, "As you know Dr. Ball will be leaving to resume a military sponsored surgical residency. You will become the chief in the flight surgeons office."

Surprised, I answered, "Sir, I'm younger than a couple of those guys in the office, so why me?"

He removed and placed his glasses on the desk, glanced at me as he leaned back in his chair. He was about six feet five and a husky guy. The hospital staff fondly called him the bear, not because he was tough, but because he was a teddy bear in the disguise of a high-ranking military officer. "You've had an extra year of general surgery. Your date of rank precedes theirs and you carry two military designations, a flight surgeon and a general

42

surgeon. You have the most medical training." He looked at me with a serious expression. "Like your predecessor, you trained at Grady in Atlanta and I'm sure or at least hope you can do as good a job as he has done."

"Thank you sir, I'll do the best I can," I was ready to leave and rose from my chair.

"Oh, and by the way, you will also be the acting psychiatrist and family counselor in the flight surgeon's office. Your predecessor did a great job counseling."

I slumped back down into my chair and shook my head in dismay. "Dr. Block, I had almost no psychiatry in med school. The dean fired the whole psychiatry department, lock stock and barrel the year I began. I barely know the definitions of all the psychiatric conditions. And, anyway, Dr. Ball is married and has four little children. He has a real family. I'm single and have no experience in marriage counseling."

I paused for a minute and looked out the window, trying to get my thoughts in order. "Just how do you counsel married people? I thought that's what the chaplains did. That will make me feel like a Catholic priest. Those guys don't know any thing about marriage and neither do I. Gee, I don't even have a steady girl friend."

He chuckled and leaned toward me, "Well, I know you are not Catholic but it's in the job description."

"It must be in the fine print," I responded.

He paused and glanced out the nearby window for a moment. It was beginning to rain. He returned to the conversation. "We've got some marriage problems on base, so get Dr. Ball to advise you about some of them before he leaves. It affects their flying performance. I know you can do it. Talk to some of the other married doctors and let them help you."

"Sir, do you think we could get a real psychiatrist for the hospital any time soon?"

"I doubt it," he answered. "We're using Philadelphia and Bethesda Naval Hospitals and Walter Reed in D.C., our referral centers, as you know, but I would hope you can handle most of the problems here. Sergeant Brewer will move your office stuff into the chief flight surgeon's office when Dr. Ball leaves. Good luck."

I again stood and thanked him for being selected as the chief, but wondered, how the other doctors would take it and how I would handle any marital difficulties on our base. We rarely saluted in the hospital. I simply acknowledged the end of the conversation and left the office.

Though I had been on the base for almost a year, I hadn't figured out all the interpersonal nuances of the base population. When I arrived my master sergeant came into my office. At first it seemed that he was my boss. He casually sat down, cigar stub in hand and began to inform me of unofficial off duty-accepted policies. He started off by asking personal questions, which I was resistant to answer.

I should be asking him those questions, I thought. "What have those questions got to do with anything?" I inquired.

He began, "There are two areas of potential problems on this base, Doc. The first is race and the second is marriage and fidelity. I know you are from the South and we have a number of "colored" corpsmen in the office. They want to know how you, a southerner, will treat them?" (The Military was racially integrated by President Truman in the mid 1940s, but the South was still in the throws of racial segregation in the early 1960s).

I looked at him, likely with a blank expression, wondering about such a question. "Well, Sergeant, you can tell them that I'll treat every body the same. If each person does his duty, we'll get along fine. If any one doesn't then I'll kick his ass out onto KP duty regardless of color or condition, as they say. Got it."

He did not seem upset by my answer, merely nodded, glanced up at the ceiling, leaned forward in his chair with no other expression apparent. He put the unlit cigar in his mouth as if he were going to take a puff and said, "Yes sir, I'm glad to hear that and I'll tell the men."

He again leaned forward in his chair and began to expound on the problems of marital fidelity. "Most of the marriages are pretty stable but, Doc, you already know that we have some, shall we say, running around of the married guys on base. Well, it's the wives running around too. There are a number of wives who, as soon as their husbands are airborne, their back doors are opened to all visitors."

He shifted in the chair, leaned back and pulled out a Zippo lighter and proceeded to light his cigar. I didn't say anything. I didn't smoke. I wanted him to be comfortable and free to talk. I wanted to hear all he had to say.

"Yes, sir, there are unofficial rules. I know you are single and I gotta' tell you there are lots of temptations out there for young bachelor officers like you, especially the younger officers with the older wives."

"How do you know all this?" I asked.

"Oh Doc, after you've been around here as long as I have you've seen it all. The rules are; first, an officer never dates an NCO or enlisted man's wife. That will get even the highest brass in deep trouble.

"Second, an officer never dates or sleeps with a lower ranked officer's wife. It just isn't acceptable. If a young lieutenant or captain has an affair with a major's wife, then it's considered fair game. If the major finds out he can get back at the young lieutenant or captain, but not the other way around. You just watch at the officer's club, you can see how they match up. Watch those officer's wives who hang around the bar when their husbands are out on flights. They won't leave together but you watch that the young guy will soon leave after the "old lady" goes out. Ask Sgt. Smith. He tends bar at the officer's club. He will point them out to you." I didn't know Sgt. Smith.

"Well, Sergeant, my job is to counsel those with marriage problems."

"Oh my, you've got a big job then." He ran his hand across his face, gesturing a concern for any positive results and fumbled with his cigar, "Dr. Ball has tried and succeeded with some, but it's hard. Lot 'a time the Air Force just transfers them, but that doesn't always solve the problems. Yes, sir, you've got a big job."

The smoke was getting thicker and I asked my sergeant to take his cigar outside. "Yes, sir, didn't know it bothered you." He slowly rose from his chair and stepped out into the clinic waiting room. He took some bandage scissors and cut the burning end off his cigar into the ashtray near the reception desk. He began to converse with the corpsmen and regular medical staff.

The enlisted corpsmen gathered about him as chicks about a mother hen. I heard him mumble, as he chewed his cigar, "Yeah, I believe we can handle this young Doc." They all peered around the door and I could see them smiling with relief.

A few days later following the conference with Colonel Block our office received a telephone call from one of the squadrons. "Hi Doc," a commanding voice boomed over the phone.

"Yes, Colonel – what can I do for you today?" I asked.

"It's one of my pilots," he said. "I'm afraid it's the pilot and his wife, that's the trouble. They're having so much difficulty that he wants to quit the Air Force because he says she is so unhappy." He paused, "Think you could come over here to the squadron and talk to me about them? He's on TDY in Rhein Maine." I could hear him ask his sergeant, "Is Major–– in Rhein Maine or Chatereaux?" He then returned to our conversation. "The rumor is she's home sleeping with a young buck, a lieutenant from another squadron."

The commander further explained. "Her husband's a career major. He has only a few years to retire. If he quits now he loses his pension. He's World War II, a good pilot with an excellent record. We hope to keep him on until retirement. We don't want to lose him. He's really important to the squadron. I suspect she's one of the reasons he was passed over for lieutenant colonel. He's in his forties and she's over ten years younger."

He continued. "If the lieutenant in question were in our squadron I could call him in and lay down the law to him. I could solve this problem, but since he's in another squadron, I can only ask his commander to help. I'm too embarrassed for our major, to ask. That's all I can say over the phone. Big problem! Think you can help us, Doc?" he again asked. "Damned if I know what to do."

"I'll come right over and we can try," I said.

A couple of days later I made a telephone call to the major's spouse. "Mrs.–– I recently spoke to your husband's squadron commander and he has asked me to talk to you here in the flight surgeon's office about you and your husband. He feels that you all have a situation which is interfering with your husband's ability to perform his duty." There was silence on the other end of the phone. "He has asked me to help you both resolve these problems."

Still, it was quiet on the other end of the line, then, "Is it really necessary that I come in to see you?" she asked.

I responded, "Yes, and this will be a confidential meeting in my office at the end of the day and only you and your husband's commander and I will be aware of our meeting. I will not have to pull your medical charts or record any of our conversation. This visit will be off the record and as I said, confidential."

Again there was a moment of silence, then I reaffirmed my concern, "Yes, ma'am, it's really important. Some times marriages and careers can be saved with honest discussions. Many problems and misunderstandings can be resolved with a little bit of effort by all parties. I will do what I can to help you both," I said. "It will be absolutely private."

She responded, "Does my husband know about this meeting?"

"I'm not sure, but I'll check with his commander," I said. "Would about four o'clock tomorrow be okay?" I asked.

"Yes, I'll be there." Her voice became softer. I thought I heard a slight Southern accent. "Thank you for calling. Maybe you can help," she sighed.

I placed the phone back on the receiver and thought, "now, what the hell do I do?"

The next day we finished the afternoon's work shortly before four o'clock. I asked one of the corpsmen to stay around until my last appointment arrived. I thought it would be proper to have at least one corpsman in the office when my major's spouse came in for her visit. He could leave shortly afterward. I didn't know her and didn't know what to expect.

At the appointed time she appeared at the office reception desk. She announced herself to the corpsman. He came into my office to notify me. "The last appointment has arrived."

The corpsman showed her into my office and I cautiously stood and greeted her. She was a "looker" as the men would say, tall, with long auburn hair, and sparkling, green eyes. I could see why all the young bachelors were interested. She held out her hand and at first I didn't know whether to shake hands or what. I fumbled with my chair and she quickly withdrew her hand. She apparently realized that this was a professional visit and we were here for serious business.

"Please have a seat," I said.

She took a seat adjacent the corner of my desk, smiled shyly, crossed her long slender legs so that her skirt fell just above her knees. Woo! Boy, I thought. This young lady is on the make, but I was wrong, sadly wrong to have judged her. She explained how unhappy she was with military life. It was not at all, as glamorous as she had expected. She had been married for about three years. She had no children from a prior marriage and she and the Major had none. "When he is gone, I'm so lonesome," she volunteered. "I don't seem to make many friends. I don't know why."

She is so good looking, I thought. I wondered, if all the other officers came on to her and perhaps their wives were jealous. I pushed my chair back and got up from my desk, opened the door, excused myself, and asked if she would like some water. I whispered to the corpsman in the waiting room, "Stay around a little longer."

I left the door ajar when I returned with glasses of water for us both. We talked for about thirty minutes and I announced to her that her husband's squadron commander had asked me to go to Chatereaux, Rhein Maine, or possibly Evereaux, whichever location he was currently assigned and discuss their marital problems and her unhappiness. She seemed agreeable to the idea that outside counseling might help.

I dared not mention the alleged affairs with the young lieutenant. She could tell me about it if she wished at a later visit. "I do love my husband," she said, "and I think he loves me. Its just so hard to be happy when he is gone so much and I am all alone."

She now had tears in her eyes. I resisted offering her a handkerchief and she opened her purse and pulled out a tissue and wiped her eyes, smudging her mascara. That done, I thanked her for coming in to the office and told her that I would like to talk to her again before I flew to Europe to discuss the matter with her husband. She agreed and thanked me for my help. She left the office.

I could not help but notice her tight skirt as she slipped out the door and I wondered, Oh, not me too? My corpsman held the door as she exited.

After a second visit with the major's spouse orders were cut for me to fly on one of our squadron planes to Europe, where his squadron had relocated. I arrived and went directly to his squadron headquarters. He was temporarily in charge of scheduling so he was on the ground and available. He was aware of my conversations with his wife. He was expecting me. We spent several hours discussing his marital situation.

He seemed embarrassed that I should have to come to his base to discuss his personal situation. "It really isn't necessary that you come all this distance," he remarked. He sat behind a paper cluttered desk in one of the private offices. I sat in a hard back chair nearby.

"Major——," I said, "you've had an outstanding career and I'm here not just to support you in your marriage, but to try to retain you in the Air Force." I paused to think for a moment. "You are needed by your squadron. According to your commander, the senior offices are concerned that you are considering leaving the military."

He tilted back in his chair, glanced up at the ceiling, then back at me, "Yeah, Doc, I know my life's a mess."

"It's not a mess, Major. I just think you and your wife need to look at your whole life style and what it will take to resolve your difficulties. I'm here to help you both." We spoke for about another hour.

He was gradually convinced that it could be worked out. He mentioned only once that he believed his wife had an affair. "The rumor is that my wife has had an affair," he murmured with what I thought were a few tears in his eyes, "I believe it is over." He didn't mention any names. He blamed her loneliness and unhappiness when he was away. He was not sure about resigning his commission.

I affirmed to him, "She has told me that she loves you and she believes you love her in return." He didn't respond and turned looking toward the closed door for a few seconds.

"Yes, maybe you're right," he said.

After a few days in Europe I returned to my base. On the first day back my sergeant came into my office, slowly and deliberately choosing his words, said to me, "The major's wife has recently been seen leaving the officer's club with the lieutenant in question." I was pissed!

The first thing I did was talk to my hospital commander to get his permission to call the lover's squadron commander. With that okay, I spoke to the commander of his squadron and asked that the lieutenant be sent to my office. "Sir," I said to the commander, "It appears that every one involved in this damn episode is too embarrassed to face the reality of the situation except me, and I will talk to the hot shot lieutenant."

The next day the young lieutenant appeared in my office. I knew him well and liked him. He was in one of my assigned squadrons and I felt if any one could talk to him, I could. He was a handsome young man and

I knew he had many girl friends. "Just one too many," I said to him, "and the wrong damn one too many." He seemed surprised that I was aware of his dalliances. He sat aloof and silent at first, his hands clasped tightly in his lap.

"You know, your commander and I have discussed transferring you to Thule, Greenland if this affair isn't ended. Up there you'll be off flying status with no flight pay and it'll be so cold you'll never unzip your damn britches," I said to him.

"Thule?" he gasped.

"Yes, Thule," I said. "Your colonel and I mean it. We suggest you pack your "muck lucks" and Arctic gear and get out of your apartment lease. You can check with the legal office to get your housing lease canceled because of transfer orders."

He looked shocked that we would suggest such a desolate and punitive assignment.

"I've had to fly all the damn way to Europe to resolve this mess you and your girl friend have created," I blurted out.

I got up from my desk and stood beside a nearby window glancing out into a cloud filled sky. "This has perhaps ruined a good officer's career." I glared at him. "Is she worth it? If she ends her marriage do you intend to marry a women ten years older than yourself?"

He sat in the chair facing my desk. He put his hands up to cover his mouth. He leaned forward, elbows on his knees, closed his eyes, shook his head and quietly responded, "You know, you are right. I'm not ready to settle down." He paused, as he sat up straight and starred passed me out the window. A grim silence filled the room. It had begun to drizzle rain. "I'll end it," he whispered.

"Now," I said.

"Yes, now."

WE CHOOSE OUR OWN POISONS

"You guys in the flight surgeons office have all the fun," complained a disgruntled clinic doctor. "All we do all day is see dependents without much wrong with them. I don't mind the kids. At least they're sick. It's the colonel and master sergeant's spouses that piss me off. They are so demanding. They complain if they have to wait and insist that their problems are special. They drive me damn crazy."

"Maybe you should have gone into psychiatry," I suggested. "Then you could understand them." He didn't think it was humorous.

"You guys fly all over the world while we're stuck in this God forsaken general clinic," he grumbled.

"We choose our own poisons," I said.

His problem was that he had gone into medicine for the wrong reasons. "My uncle in the Bronx makes ten times as much," he complained. The guy simply resented being in the service rather than a big money practice.

It was true that we had more fun treating the flying personnel. When our office clinic became tiresome we could check the rotation schedule and when our rotation time came we could call our squadrons and check to see what was going out. We tried to keep at least one or occasionally two flight surgeon out on the line.

Mostly they called us to notify us of their need for a flight surgeon to accompany flights in special conditions. That meant the guys assigned to the airlift squadrons could fly all over the globe. The men of the squadrons loved to have the flight surgeon flying with them. It was part of working together and acquiring the squadron's confidence. It was essential that the flying personnel have assurance in their flight surgeon's personal interest and that they felt free to honestly discuss any problems with their docs. We were their priests in white.

Those of us assigned to a fighter squadron could fly in supersonic planes just for fun. We were delighted when the operation officers or the squadron commander called, "Hey Doc, would you like to fly in the back seat today?"

"You bet, sir," we most always answered. We flew routine flights as well as high altitude flights.

We invited select members of the hospital staff physicians to go through the altitude chamber and fly with the squadrons, particularly the cardiologists. They helped us with routine and special diagnostic evaluations of heart problems that might affect the ability of the men on flying status to perform their flight duties.

As good physicians as the general medical and surgery officers were, yet they never understood the potential dangers of flying. They never had to investigate crash sites in which their flying friends might be involved. They never had the heart wrenching job of collecting the remains or ashes of their friends. As I said to the other docs, "We choose our own poisons."

KNEW HOW THEY FELT

Thursday was squadron physical exam day in the flight surgeon's office when squadron members on flying status assembled for their annual physicals. A line of enlisted airmen stood at rest in the office for their exams. I walked down the line of young men, looked them over standing in their shorts and bare feet, examined them, first head and upper body, checked their eyes, ears, throats, and necks for any masses or unusual findings. I pulled out my stethoscope and listened to their chests for heart and lung abnormalities. All seemed okay.

I walked down the line changing gloves at each man and checking them for hernias or scrotal masses. "Cough" I ordered and as they did I felt the inguinal areas. Then I ordered "Drop your shorts all the way down." I walked behind each and when I came to the third or fourth airman I mechanically and boringly asked, "Lean over, spread your cheeks and say Ahh!" With that I paused and thought, damn, I've just lost my mind. I'm at the wrong end for ahhs. I shook my head and turned to my assisting corpsman, "Ask one of the other docs to finish this damn exam. I've had it." Suddenly I understood the general clinic doctor's complaints.

In my office I picked up my hat, and headed for the officers club for a beer. "I need a break, office fatigue," I mumbled to the NCO in charge and I was gone.

HIGH FLYING

"… a hazy fog…"

The men filed out of the 98th briefing room after receiving their instructions and schedules for the day. "Oh, Doc," Major Chappy called out. "I need to see you in my office."

"Sure Chappy," I said. I had a few words with a couple of the pilots and navigators and headed down the bright hall to the Operations Office.

"Col. Crain has set up a schedule for you and a couple of the men to go to Wright-Patterson to be fitted for high altitude suits. Since you'll be taking over the Squadron as our doc, Col. Crain wants you to participate in the high altitude flights." Chappy paused, "He feels you'll be more aware of the potential problems that the guys sometime have with the pressure suits. Occasionally the they feel closed in when they are at altitude and the plane decompresses and the pressure suit inflates. He thinks you can help with any psychological fears that the men might have if you have experienced the decompressions yourself."

I was surprised at this comment and wasn't sure if the other flight surgeons had been fitted or not. "I'll have to check with the hospital before I go."

"Oh, we've already talked to them and you will be relieved of your office duties while you are out in Dayton."

"When will we go and who will be going with me?" I inquired.

He named a couple of pilots and navigators. "Your commercial flight tickets will be sent to your office, so don't plan anything for the next week or so."

The commercial flight to Dayton was unremarkable. We were generously served strong drinks by the flight attendants. "I'm told we ought not to have any thing strong to drink, no alcohol for at least twelve hours before we are fitted and put in the decompression chamber," I announced.

The officers seemed surprised, smiled slyly, and glanced at each other, "Ah Doc, you know we would never break those rules."

"Of course not," I answered.

Wright Patterson is the scientific heart of the Air Force. The Air Force Institute of Technology is located there. A sergeant from the motor pool met us at the airport and drove us to the officer's transient quarters. "We'll pick you up tomorrow at 0700 for your fitting, sir."

The fitting area looked like a Sears and Roebuck with racks of all the unimaginable clothing and more flight equipment than I had ever seen. We were stripped to our shorts and socks, measured and weighed. Then the slow process began. "Sir, we get all kind of folks to fit for these suits, some thin and some fat, so it may take a few hours getting done," said the fitting airman.

Several partial pressure suits were tried using a lacing process to get the perfect fit. It felt like a bear hug. I knew how Scarlet O'Hara felt when "Mammy" in Gone With the Wind, laced her tight corset. We could move with the strangest flexing and extension of our limbs. "You know we've got to fit the flight boots over these pants," the fitting airman grunted as he pulled the lacing tighter about the suit.

The attached soft hoods were fitted and we could see our selves in the nearby mirrors like mummies in olive drab suits. "The capstans inflate on decompression," he explained. The capstans were inflatable, cylindrical, rubber lined, cloth tubes that ran along the trunk, the sleeves and pants. Upon activation of compressed air from an attached pressure cylinder the tubes expand, stiffening the arms so that the airman is barely able to flex or extend his arms, but is protected from the outside low atmospheric pressure. The ability of each individual to move and function is carefully measured and evaluated.

Once fitted with a protective helmet, slipped over the hood and the clear plastic face mask tightly positioned, we were ready for the altitude decompression chamber. The officer, in charge explained that the airtight decompression chamber is a large metal tank with windows through which the trained technicians are able to watch and monitor the airman in the chamber.

The atmospheric pressure is initially calibrated to sea level and the altitude chamber is gradually decompressed simulating a rise to altitude. Without any change in the suit, the pressure is dropped gradually to the equivalent of 30,000 feet altitude. The airman is able to communicate through a face microphone within the helmet unit with the chamber technicians. A manometer is located inside the chamber so that it can be monitored inside and the altitude (pressure) gages can be observed from exterior into the chamber.

We observed that once the technician drops the pressure precipitously, the chamber fills with a hazy fog. The pressure is adjusted to the equivalent altitude greater than 50,000 feet and the partial-pressure suit inflates. It is a sudden compression of the whole body, arms and legs. Inside the hood and helmet the airman can feel little difference. The individual in the chamber is observed for any defects in the suit's performance and any physiological as well as any psychological mal-effects.

Assuming all systems are okay the chamber pressure is slowly adjusted to ground level after a few minutes and the airman is removed from the chamber. The aviator must be able to move arms and legs and communicate as if he or she were in an in-flight configuration, able to reach, touch, and handle controls that would be present in the actual aeroplane.

It took a couple of days to be properly fitted. The physiology sergeant explained the limitations of the suit. "If you gain more than four to six pounds, the suit will be too tight and if you lose four to six pounds the suit will be too loose to function properly. It will have to be re-laced and refitted. At your base you will be weighed and measured regularly or at most each time you are suited up for your flights."

He further reminded us that these partial pressure suits were to be used exclusively for flights that would be at altitudes over 50,000 to 60,000 feet. (These partial pressure suits predated the full pressure suits that would be worn by later astronauts). The DuPont Company in Delaware designed and developed several versions of the full pressure suits.

The so-called partial pressure suit was the model worn by U-2 pilot Gary Powers. While on a spy flight (CIA) over the Soviet Union, during the Eisenhower Administration. He was shot down by Soviet antiaircraft missiles. The incident led to further strains in American-Soviet relations, a cancellation of a major Soviet-American conference and an intensification of the Cold War.

We were glad to know that the partial pressure suit had saved Power's life. He had been flying at a classified altitude of over 100,000, feet. When his plane was hit he ejected and free fell thousands of feet before his safety parachute opened. The suit was also later worn by U-2 pilots over Cuba. The suits were worn by all U-2 pilots.

We had only a few problems with the pressure suits at our base. Several pilots and radar observers complained that when the airplane was at high altitude, they worried that their suits might not inflate. It was necessary for me to fly at the classified high altitudes to test the suits.

To perform the test, the pilot reached the desired altitude, leveled the plane and prepared to dive at the moment the plane decompressed and the suit was tested. I could report to the crew members that I had experienced no difficulty with the suit and that the suit inflated properly and reassured them of the safety of their suits and equipment.

High Altitude Chamber – Wright-Patterson AFB – Dayton, Ohio

"Once the altitude pressure is dropped the chamber fills with a hazy fog."

Note: the pressure gages inside the chamber.

OCTOBER 20, 1962

Dover Air Force Base

The Thirty First Air Transport Squadron's promotion party was scheduled to begin at twenty-hundred hours (8:00 p.m.) at the Officers Club. Many of the second lieutenants would change their single gold bar for a first lieutenant's silver one and those who were promoted to captain would add another silver bar. I was not among those promoted. I entered the military with two silver bars, much to the chagrin of my pilot and navigator friends.

"Officers and Their Ladies," the printed squadron invitation said. Who should I ask? Who would be tolerant enough for what I knew would be a rowdy affair before the evening was over. My little black address book was not exactly full. It was far from being filled. I asked my pals at our house if they had any suggestions. As an itinerant traveler, I had recently moved into another bachelor house known as the "Lake House."

They were all dashing flyers, handsome and daring, at least that's what they thought. But, would they share?

Well, they "might share with their flight surgeon buddy," they said, "but he couldn't lay any claim on his date after the party was over."

That seemed reasonable to me. I was not interested in any long-term affair, just a date. I remembered my mother telling me once when one of her friends had a daughter with that cliché, a wonderful personality, "You don't have to marry everyone you ever date."

I wasn't as dashing as all my flying pals. I didn't fly the plane. I didn't navigate the plane. I just decided from a medical standpoint, who could fly and navigate the plane. That gave me some kind of authority that I didn't understand for a long time.

I asked my hospital commander about these promotion parties. He explained, "The squadron's flight surgeon always attends the parties to support the aircrews." It was hoped that the squadron would see that the "Doc" was one of them. "Of course," he said, "the doctor should remain the soberest of the crowd and not bring embarrassment on the flight surgeon's office."

He didn't need to worry. One of my favorite corpsman was an after hours bartenders and I had advised Sergeant Kafel, "Never let me over indulge regardless of how much I have to drink with my flying crews." He was to spike my drinks with water when necessary so that at least, I could walk upright out of the bar. I didn't know what my tolerance might be. This allowed me to stand elbow to elbow at the bar with those of my squadrons as they rolled dice for drinks at Happy Hour. I never knew if he spiked my drinks or not. He never volunteered and I never asked.

Col. Strong had been a medical officer and an established figure at the hospital and on the base. He was a regular at the officers club. He was not shy about cutting in on the younger officers dates. He admired beautiful women. My pals warned me about his "bird dogging." I came to know him and liked him and respected him professionally.

Once while driving to the Delaware shore I spotted a shiny, blue, Corvette convertible in my rear view mirror. It sped by me, leaving me in its exhaust. A gray haired gent waved his checkered hat as he passed. That was Col. Strong. Unfortunately, life caught up with him and he died suddenly from a massive stroke.

My hospital commander requested that I accompany him to visit the family of the said deceased officer to pay our respects and represent the medical section of the base. There I met his adult daughter, the "lovely Millie" as my friends called her. She sat quietly with her mother. Millie was about 5 feet 4, slender, with soft blonde hair, tightly pulled back, and piercing sparkling blue eyes. She spoke softly. She and her mother disguised their grief with remarkable military stoicism.

When I inquired about that certain young lady, my commander commented, "It would be proper courtesy to invite the late Colonel Strong's daughter to the promotion party."

Millie dated a number of my fellow airmen before I came to the base. I was hesitant to invite her to the promotion party for fear of stepping on one of my squadron member's toes. It was so soon after her father's death, I wondered if it was appropriate. I learned in no time, "partying" in the Air Force stood on little ceremony. Yes, she would go. I even asked her mother. She agreed, "It would be good for Millie to get back into the social life of the base." A visit to the officers club would be just the thing, since adult dependents lost their privileges to the Club after the death of the military parent. She would go as my guest or my "Lady" in this case.

We arrived at the Club before the party, my date in a loose, light blue, fall, dress, complimenting my military blues and her blonde hair and blue eyes. We had cocktails and dinner with a number of the other young "Officers and their Ladies."

With all fully imbibed, the party became boisterously loud with singing at the bar, crap shooting over in the dark corners, dice rollers on their knees, ties loosened, jackets unbuttoned, and ladies holding up their officers on the dance floor, the music reverberated through out the club.

Without warning, the squadron commander stepped up on the band stand, replaced the band leader, and took the microphone. "Attention, attention," he said. The music stopped, the dancers turned to the podium on which Col. Cupko stood. Blurry eyes turned in his direction. "Attention," he said again. "It's been a great party and I'm sorry to have to announce that our celebration will end at midnight for those on flying status. Each of you on flying status must report to Base Ops at 0500 with tropical gear for an extended mission. I can't give any details, but report first to Base Supply to receive, helmets, flack jackets and appropriate weapons. Bring all your flying charts, landing plates and necessary personal equipment. Remember, tropical gear."

"Oh yes," he said, "congratulations to the newly promoted officers. That is all. No questions." He paused for a moment then stepped down from the podium. The room remained ominously silent for a couple of minutes. The band started up again with a slow number until the party of those not on flying status reengaged in the celebration.

Shortly before midnight my date and I left the Officers Club and walked out into the dark and foggy parking lot. It was not unusual to have cold and fog in October so close to the Eastern shore. A few of the squadron members were standing around sobering up in the brisk night air. It was difficult to see the smoke from their cigarettes for the fog.

We wondered what the weather would have in store in just a few hours. Would the fog lift long enough to allow takeoffs or would we be delayed? We knew we were going out by 0800 or 0900. I remembered the rule, "No alcohol within eight hours of flight." Looking around I wondered if that meant only, "No alcohol within eight feet of the airplane." We had no firm orders and would get those at Base Ops in the dark early morning when we arrived. The aircraft commanders would first be briefed about our destination, then the rest of the crews.

We bade our friends good night and drove slowly away from the club into the dense fog, watching the center yellow line of the road, leaning out the door, since we could see only a few feet in front of the car. "I will stay at your house," volunteered Millie, "to be sure you make it to the Base." She lived only a few blocks from my house on the small lake, near the air base. As a "military brat" she understood how it all worked. To be late or miss a scheduled flight was to be in big trouble. It could mean a reprimand or even a court-martial. I was not ready for either.

"I'll drive you to the base and bring your car home," said Millie. "You need to get some sleep."

In the living room we built a fire in the great stone fireplace. Soon the fire was blazing and crackling with flames from the dry hickory logs. The light danced on the walls like little Indians making their war chant, whooping it up about a bonfire. It was cozy and warm near the fire. Millie went into the kitchen and soon returned with steaming hot chocolate. "Something to warm us up," she quietly said.

We decided to stay in the living room, now the only warm room in the house. Millie, dressed in a pair of my rolled up pajamas, reclined on the sofa with an old army cover and a pillow from my room. I found a place on a sleeping bag close to the fire. I had almost four hours to rest before starting a big day with my squadron. I wasn't thinking so much about tomorrow. I was just thinking about resting for a little while.

Despite the warm fire, the distant part of the room felt chilled. Millie slipped from the sofa and gently tiptoed across the room in the shimmering shadows of the fire, toward the warm hearth. She knelt beside me, placed the old Army comfort over us, placed her soft head on my shoulder and whispered, "Get some sleep soldier, tomorrow's a long day." We watched the glowing fire as we dozed off.

Lake House" on Moore's Lake Dover, Delaware, 1962 – 1963

"We watched the glowing fire as we dozed off."

OCTOBER 21, 1962

At 0400 the clanging of the red wind up Big Ben alarm clock startled me. The fire had burned down. Only the soft sparkling glow of the ashes and an occasional small slender flame remained. A chill was again in the air. I peered out the window into the still, dark morning. All I could see was the fog rolling in from the lake up the shallow, frosty, hill upon which we lived. A small hazy halo of light was barely visible at the end of our narrow dock. It was peaceful outside our little world. I stoked the fire and added a small log. I needed to get some warmth back in the room. From the kitchen I heard a soft voice, "I've got the coffee perking and I'll have some eggs and toast ready. Go ahead and shower. Remember, Col. Cupko said tropical clothes and gear. I was glad I had invited this girl to the party.

Might as well take the Arctic gear from my travel bag and add some more appropriate tropical stuff, I thought. I kept an extra travel bag in the trunk of my car. I might be called at any time at home or at the hospital to report for an unscheduled flight.

Millie dropped me off at Base Supply, blew a kiss over her fingertips and bid me, "Be careful. Come back safely." She would check with the flight surgeons office or the ops office about our return.

The crew members gathered to receive their tropical equipment. I could separate the partygoers from those who had not been at the promotion party, simply by smell. I hoped none of these guys would be flying or in charge of flying that day. The airmen and officers were not separated as we moved through the supply line. Two airmen nearby were bright eyed and spoke about a possible adventure. "Man, do you really think all this means real war?" one whispered to his buddy. The older sergeants and officers were more relaxed as this was routine for them. It was however, a sudden "Alert." Even the old veterans seemed to know something unusual was up.

The line eased forward dragging duffle and travel bags. "Move on," one sergeant growled at the airman in front of him, who appeared wavering in the line. The issuing airman asked each of us if we had certain items for tropical duty. Quinine tablets, to prevent malaria, were handed out in waterproof packages, by a hospital corpsman that was assisting the supply staff.

We moved down the line. The supply sergeant handed me a helmet with a medical cloth cover. The next sergeant wrote down a serial number and handed me a form, "Sign here." He pointed to the crumpled yellow paper. He then placed on the counter a khaki .45 caliber Colt pistol, a couple of cartridge clips, and holster.

"Wait a minute," I said to him. "I'm a healer, not a fighter and I don't think a medic is supposed to have a weapon, according to the Geneva Convention." He looked at me with an odd frown. He glanced at my helmet then the flight surgeon's wings on my flight jacket.

"Hell, Doc, those guys out there think the cross on that helmet is a target." He nodded.

"Take it, Sir. Hope you don't need it." He moved to the next man.

Our squadron assembled in Base Ops. "Go to the briefing room and connect with Captain Oehmey," a gruff major said to me. I was pleased with that name.

"He's a good officer," an airmen said, "and he's a no-nonsense aircraft commander."

The Operations Officer pointed to a large map at the rear of the briefing room. All I could see was the Southeastern United States and the island of Cuba. "Gentlemen," he said, "you, and your crews, will be ferried by aircraft to this point." He paused, "Charleston." He pointed his stick to a spot in South Carolina. "You will remain here until your squadron's aircraft return from the West Coast. You will replace those crews. Those planes will be refueled and you will fly the planes to our Naval base at Guantanamo Bay, Cuba. Charleston will supply you with landing plates and further instructions."

The major looked about the room at the assembled crews and raised his voice; "The Fifteenth Squadron flew your planes to Camp Pendleton in California yesterday and picked up the Combat Ready Marines. You will fly them and their equipment, ammunition and weapons, to your assigned destination. You will receive more information about the threatening situation in Cuba before you take off. Remember, our commanders and our President consider this mission as urgent." He paused, "No questions, please."

We arrived at the Charleston Air Base. A crew rest was ordered. No one could leave the local air base, under penalty of arrest. We were to eat, rest, and check our equipment. One young lieutenant mumbled to his cohort, "I got an old girl friend in Charleston and I sure would like to get off base, just long enough to see her."

"Hell, you'll be in a lot of damn trouble if you even try, you dumb ass," his pal replied.

Pilots and navigators reported to preflight briefings, reviewed their flight charts, and received specific instructions concerning their mission. They were given special landing plate instructions.

When I returned to our assigned quarters from the evening meal, someone had disassembled my .45 pistol and left all the parts scrambled in disarray on my cot. Several of the officers ignored the pile of parts and with sly smiles watched to see what I would do or say.

"Oh, look what Doc has on his bed," one of them glibly said. They all gathered about my bunk.

"Damn," I said, "looks like it all fell apart. What kind of weapons are they handing out these days?" They began to shake their heads and softly laugh. No one offered to help.

"Well, Doc told them he wasn't supposed to have a gun, said it was against Geneva Rules," one young second lieutenant chimed in.

Before the joke and laughter became too loud, I sat down on my bed and began to line the pieces and parts in an organized pile. "What's next Doc?" one of the bright young lieutenants smirked.

"Guess I'll have to reassemble it." They laughed in disbelief. I picked up the pieces and began to put the weapon back together. As I finished, I checked the chamber, removed the clip and shells, looked down the barrel, cocked the gun, and clicked it several times toward the ceiling.

"Damn, He did it," said one of the pilots. "I'll just be damned." I was now one of them.

OCTOBER 22, 1962

I never told them that before I entered the service, a family friend, a retired infantry officer gave me his .45 that he had used in the China-Burma-India Theater, during World War ll and later in Korea. He taught me to disassemble, clean and reassemble that specific weapon. We hoped I would never have to use it. Now, I hoped I would never have to use the one on my bunk.

The Duty sergeant awakened us at 0500 and announced that our planes had returned from the West Coast, were being refueled, and would be prepared for us to replace the crews by 0800. We showered, gathered up our equipment, including our side arms, picked up coffee and a quick hot meal at a portable kitchen and assembled for our crew instructions.

We were taken to the waiting Globemasters by blue crew buses and we boarded our planes. Capt. Oehmey, the aircraft commander greeted me, "Doc, you sit up front with us so you can see what is going on."

It dawned on me that this whole business was for real. This was not an exercise. The bit of anxiety melted into a feeling of excitement and high adventure. I felt calm as I moved about the cockpit. So this is what it is like to go into serious military action, I thought.

Capt. Oehmey leaned over from the left pilot seat, holding out some landing plates and pointed to the runway, commented to the copilot, "I've reviewed the landing instructions and think the instructions at the briefing would make the directed down wind turn too tight to land safely at Leeward Point." He commented, "We'll be flying over Cuban territory. We'll have to come down beyond the boundary of the base and will be over a section of Cuba." He paused, "Hell, we'll be within their defendable territory by international law." He paused. "They have the right to fire on our planes for penetrating their sovereign territory."

He again turned to the copilot, "That turn is just too darn tight," he added. "We'll have to veer over the line any way. If they object, we'll just have to take that chance." He turned from the left pilot's seat toward me and again said, "Hey, Doc, Come up here and sit. We have steel armor plates under this section of the crew compartment. It'll be safe if there is any ground fire."

"At least it will keep us safe from getting hit in the ass," blurted out the flight engineer from across the cockpit.

I gulped, frowned at him and mumbled, "Damn, this thing is for real, isn't it?"

APPROACH

It was in a clear blue sky, except for a few puffy higher clouds as we approached Leeward Point. I could see many airplanes on the ground unloading supplies for the military detachment at Guantanamo. The planes were landing, unloading, and taking off with minimal ground time. Our plane was the first of our squadron. My orders were to stay on the ground for the duration of the airlift until all our planes had completed their shuttles. I was to go in with the first plane and return with the last plane out. Those were always my orders.

We made a wide sweep extending beyond our boundary line, crossed a long open field before the runway, dropped suddenly and touched down at Guantanamo's Leeward Point, taxied off the runway and shut down the engines. The ground crews hurried to unload our plane. There were two options to unload the plane. One was for heavy equipment from the forward part through the open clam shell doors and the second by a mid-plane elevator holding lighter cargo.

My feet hardly touched the ground, when a lean Navy lieutenant approached me, "Hey, are you the doctor for this crew? We heard one was coming," he yelled over the roar of the groaning engines nearby.

"Yeah, I am," I responded. "Why?" (Always, ask why?)

"We need you at the Base Operations Terminal" he said. We briskly crossed the tarmac, dodging a couple of small vehicles piled up with cargo, just offloaded from nearby planes and walked into the gray building, "Over here," he said, and pointed to some white curtains hanging in the flight terminal, surrounding a group of women and children. "These are the dependents waiting for evacuation. These women are pregnant and you will have to take care of them," he announced.

I looked over the throng of big tummies and little kids scurrying around the piled up luggage and duffle bags. "Wait a minute, I'm the flight surgeon. I'm not a damn obstetrician. Where are your regular Navy doctors?" I asked.

"They are out in the field with the Marines and hey, you're all we've got." He grinned and I could tell he was giving me the business. This was his playing field, not mine. "In here are a couple of nurses and corpsmen," he added. "You're it, Doc." He again pointed toward the dependents. "Our chief medical officer said to get one of the Air Force guys to take care of these folks 'till they get loaded to go. Oh yeah, we've got a delivery room set up behind these other curtains if needed."

"I haven't delivered a baby in three years, I'm a general surgeon," I protested.

"Doc, you are still it," he responded, trying to repress a silly grin.

I walked over to the first group and glanced around at the nervous but quiet potential new mothers with their children and thought; I hope I can get through this. I started talking to each woman, getting a history and inquiring about her date of confinement, or estimated delivery date. A couple of the women were "due soon" and a couple more were "overdue." I wondered, how overdue? Wow! I thought, Lord, just help me get these folks safely on their planes and out of here.

To those that were sitting I kept saying, "Keep your knees together, mama and you can get out of here okay." I didn't know what else to say. For those that were standing with children and bags, I conjured up some nearby wandering sailors to hustle them out toward the waiting C-130s and corralled some more sailors to carry the little children and baggage.

"Get all that luggage," I yelled at sailors. I couldn't believe I was ordering the Navy around. I thought I was going to war not the obstetric ward. A few of the dependent's husbands were standing nearby and began to tote bags and children to the waiting planes. A couple of the little kids were hanging onto their dad's shoulders and were excited and pointing toward the noisy planes nearby.

We got the last of the mothers, children and other non-essential civilian dependents on board the waiting C-130s. The crews slammed and locked the doors, revved up the huge four-blade propeller engines, began to move cautiously among the other transports, entered and sped down the runway, and were soon airborne. "Thank you, Lord," I said aloud. "Thank you."

The sailors standing around me gave a big cheer. They had done their job. With a couple of nurses aboard and obstetrical medical kits, the dependents were safely on their way back home to the States. The Navy Duty Officer sauntered over to me and commented, "That wasn't so bad was it, Doc?"

"No, not so bad," I responded with a feeling of relief.

"Now I can take you to your quarters." We hopped into a dusty, gray Navy jeep and headed a few hundred yards to a low slung, two story, white cinder block building, the Officers Quarters. I remembered why I liked working with the Navy, real beds with crisp white sheets, even in the worst locations. He directed me to a room and I put down my khaki travel bag, removed my helmet, laid my holstered gun on the bed and looked out the window.

The officer excused himself. "Oh yes," he said, "the password is Blue Note," or it sounded to me like he said something like that.

Flight Engineer at the plane's control panel

"Leeward Point, Guantanamo runway in sight..."

On the runway at Leeward Point.

Leeward Point – C-124s delivering ammunition and matériel.

The military C-130 began loading the evacuating dependents.

AFTERNOON

The sun was slipping toward the horizon as I peered out the window. The shadows were falling across piled up sand bags and tin roofing, covered by more sand bags, that was a machine gun-bunker, right out my window, not twenty or thirty yards away. There were several marines, sleeves cut off, with flack jackets on and their helmets sitting on nearby sand bags. They were digging more trenches about their bunker.

"Hey guys, what are you doing?" I leaned and yelled out my open window.

"Sir, we're just digging in," they said, as they briefly leaned on their shovels in the still, hot afternoon sun.

I looked out beyond the bunker and saw a heavy "barbed wire" fence, strung some fifty yards away, that I assumed was their defense perimeter. After a bit of bantering with the young marines, I asked as I pointed in the distance. "What should I do if the bad guys come through that fence?"

"Hell, Doc, just get under your bunk and we'll take care of you." The lance corporal yelled back. He patted his rifle and pointed to the machine gun emplacement.

"Damn right," I responded, "I like that." They were all smiles. I liked that Marine's attitude as much as I liked the crisp, cool white sheets.

That afternoon we settled into a routine airlift with no major problems. "We are going over to the Officers Mess, to the bar," said a tall, obviously Southern, soft-spoken Navy officer in my building, and invited me to go along.

I met and joined several other Navy and Air Force officers involved in the airlift. We sat outside on the veranda. Now a slight breeze replaced the humid air, a breeze from the nearby beach. "This is the time, in the evening when the breeze used to bring the old sailing ships to shore, but you Air Force guys wouldn't know about that," one gestured.

The sun was further settling along the horizon. Several men were gathered about a radio and others had a small black and white television set that they were setting up, adjusting the aluminum foil attached to the shiny rabbit ears antenna, trying to get a Miami station. "The President is making a speech to the country," one fellow said. Between the radio and the poorly receiving T.V. we were able to hear his speech. The gathering of men were thoughtfully silent as President Kennedy addressed the nation.

A newspaper later reported, "At 7 p.m. Monday, October 22, 1962, President Kennedy appeared on television to inform Americans of the recently discovered Soviet military buildup in Cuba, including the ongoing installation of offensive nuclear missiles."

Each of us listened intently to his message about the nuclear weapons and offensive rockets that had already been installed in Cuba by the Soviets. I felt a hint of anxiousness as he spoke. What is really going on? I wondered. Here we were, sitting ducks on the South portion of Cuba and had no idea what was in fact, going on. It seems when someone is in the middle of a major event that he or she rarely understands the significant dangers or historical importance of the event until long afterwards.

The president described our intelligence and our aerial reconnaissance of the missile sites.* He depicted the history of the deception, the secret buildup, and the danger it represented to our country. He stated he was ordering continued surveillance of Cuba, and was ordering a Naval quarantine ** of Cuban waters to prevent further introduction of offensive missiles.

He declared that any nuclear missile launched from Cuba against any nation in the Western Hemisphere would be regarded as an attack by the Soviet Union on the United States and would result in a full retaliatory response upon the Soviet Union. It was not publicly known that the United States had a far superior number of nuclear weapons than the Soviet Union. It has since been reported that the Soviets, however knew.

He further stated: "As a necessary military precaution, I (the President) have reinforced our base at Guantanamo and today have evacuated the dependents of our personnel, and ordered additional military units to be on a standby alert."

We looked at each other and murmured, "He is talking about us." We drank our cold beer, got up, now more determined by the president's strong speech and returned to our quarters.

*Major Rudolf Anderson was wearing the "partial pressure suit" over Cuba when his U-2 was shot down while on a high altitude recognizance flight during the missile crisis. He was unable to eject from his airplane. He was the first casualty of the Missile Crisis.

** Years later, interviews with Ted Sorenson, White House speech writer for President Kennedy explained that the word "quarantine" was preferred by Kennedy over the stronger belligerent term "blockade" as being too militarily aggressive. Only the newspapers and other non-government persons referred to the isolation of Cuba as a "blockade."

By late dusk I was hungry and left the officer's quarters to head for the flight line and the mobile kitchen. The air traffic had diminished. Our squadrons from EASTAF (Eastern Air Transport) were refueling in the States. Most of our aircraft would begin arriving at daylight the following day. Thus far, our planes had performed well without significant delays or incidents.

Many of the larger aircraft had difficulty on the short landing strip of Leeward Point. The planes touched down, reversed engines and attempted to brake. Great billows of smoke came from the tires as they skidded on the runway, burning the tires until many had blowouts before coming to a stop. Several teams of ground mechanics were busy changing and replacing the tires on a number of the planes as they offloaded.

By 2200 I left Base Terminal and headed back to the officers quarters. A complete blackout was in effect. I could not see more than a few feet in any direction. The only lights burning were on the runway for urgent air traffic. Unloading the aircraft in the dark was a problem, especially the boxes of explosives.

About half way back to my quarters, a shadow appeared from the darkness and a high-pitched voice summoned, "Who goes there?" I gave my name and rank. That was not enough. The sentry wanted to hear the password.

Damn, I thought. I couldn't remember what I was told. I responded, "Blue or black something."

"Sir, if you are an officer, you should know the pass word," a young, shaky, voice responded from the dark.

I told him I was a captain, and he had the impression that I meant a navy captain. When he shined his dim flashlight on me he knew I was too young to be a navy captain. "Sailor, I just came on the base," I answered. "I'm Air Force. Sorry, I don't remember the pass word."

"I'll have to take you in sir," the young sentry mumbled.

"Okay, just don't shoot me by mistake," I said, "you guys may need me." He did not respond. He nervously pointed the way with his rifle.

The sailor marched me at bayonet and gunpoint back to Base Operations. When my new acquaintance, the Navy duty officer saw us he began laughing. "Where in hell did you get this guy?" he asked the sentry.

"He didn't know the password, sir," said the young sailor.

"Good damn job sailor," said the Navy lieutenant, "he's dangerous. He's one of those Air Force guys." He shook his head in disbelief, "He's okay. He's just lost. Will you escort him to his quarters and see that he stays inside till dawn, and give him the password. We don't want any Air Force casualties on our hands."

"Yes, sir," said the sentry.

As we left the building he apologetically said, "Sorry about that. Our sentries are usually marines, but they are out in the field, so we navy men have to do the security duty for now," he proudly announced.

In my heart I smiled. These young guys are so intense in doing their duty. "Sailor, you were exactly right in doing your duty. You need not be sorry. Next time I will remember the password."

"Get under your bunk Doc."

OCTOBER 23, 1962

By daylight the air traffic increased. Larger planes from McGuire, big C-135's brought in weapons, ammunition, mortar grenades, mortar flares, and other materiel. One of our pilots was fuming mad when he landed, complaining that unlike the other transports that delivered weapons, he had brought only "tents and tent stubs," with his construction equipment. This day was to be a long one.

I checked at Base Ops for the day's roster and schedule of my squadron's arrivals. "Your flights will follow the larger planes from McGuire since those require more time and distance to land, maneuver on the ground, unload, and take off," advised the ops officer. I stayed on the flight line as planes landed, off loaded, taxied out, and took off again for another shuttle run from the States. The larger planes continued to land, and many had tires replaced as they blew out on the short runway.

The big C-135 jets all seemed to have difficulty negotiating the down wind turn that our aircraft commander had mentioned. Most of them elected, it seemed, from our vantage point to make the wide turn he had suggested, even though it was over Cuban territory beyond the open fields, distant to the runway.

A Navy lieutenant and I sat on the edge of the tarmac in the same gray jeep that had carried me to my quarters the afternoon before. We were observing the flight line activity. We relaxed under the canvass roof of our jeep, protected from the heat of the early afternoon sun. "You like a cigarette?" he asked.

"Thanks, anyway, I don't smoke." He lit his cigarette, leaned back in his seat and casually exhaled his blue smoke away from the Jeep.

In the distance I noticed one of the big C-135s began to make its down wind turn from our right to the left. The turn seemed awfully sharp, much closer than I had observed the other planes make. It looked like he was turning in slow motion. The silhouette of the plane appeared to be dipping the port (left) wing too steeply. It seemed to stop, suspended in mid air, and began to slide to the left, with the wing still dipping further toward the ground. I thought I heard a change or higher pitch in the sound of the engines as if the engines were being throttled. The plane further dipped to its left, far from the end of the runway.

Then we saw it happen. The plane simply tumbled to the ground with a huge explosion followed by a gigantic ball of golden, red flame, then dark, black smoke bellowed beyond the active runway.

We were frozen with the image of the horrible explosion. We stared at each other for a split second and without a word the Navy lieutenant flipped his cigarette out of the Jeep, and started the Jeep's motor. We darted toward the black smoke and traveled along the edge of the Leeward Point runway. We speeded up and headed directly to the downed plane. Suddenly we realized that the emergency fire trucks were following us to the crash site. We ran off the end of the runway into a cleared dirt field toward the plane just short of a mine field, at that moment unknown to us. By now flames engulfed the fuselage. We could see only the nose and the windows of the cockpit, some fifty yards ahead.

We stopped the Jeep, jumped out and ran closer to the wreckage. In the distance a sailor rushed toward us. "I was at the nose, at the cockpit," he yelled. "No survivors." He had been fishing just beyond the runway on the waters edge. He was the first person to the plane. We approached the nose but could not see inside. The cockpit of the fuselage was turned lying on its left side. The plane likely crashed with the left wing hitting the ground first.

"Then we saw it happen. The plane simply tumbled to the ground with a huge explosion followed by a gigantic ball of golden, red flame, then dark, black smoke."

"We headed directly to the downed plane…
We could see only the windows of the cockpit."

THE CRASH SITE

The sailor was singed from the intense heat generated from the fire. He ran toward us repeating, "No survivors, nobody" he yelled. "I looked in before it blew up," he cried out.

We were within twenty yards of the plane's nose. It began exploding within the midst of the fire. It was completely engulfed in flames. With the sailor we ran back toward the Jeep.

Fire trucks arrived and the firemen scurried to get their hoses set. The flames were so intense and the explosions so terrific that they abandoned the first fire truck. In addition to the burning plane and the surrounding ground fire, huge explosions occurred within the fuselage. The munitions were now exploding.

We fell to the ground, perhaps knocked down by the explosions, but I don't remember. We crawled away on our hands and knees from the crash, clawing the ground getting away. Shells and mortars were exploding. Now behind the trucks, we looked up and saw one of the fire trucks hit by what must have been a mortar shell. It burst into flames. Black smoke enveloped the truck. Something was going over our heads. It must have been more mortar rounds. We raised ourselves up from the ground, "Run, Doc, run," yelled the lieutenant. The Navy officer, the sailor and I ran to the abandoned Jeep, got it started, and left the area.

We headed back across the field to the end of the runway. At what we thought was a safe distance we stopped, turned and viewed the crash site. It was surreal. The explosions continued during the afternoon until all remnants of the plane and its contents were gone. There were no survivors of a crew of perhaps eight men. We sent the sailor to the first-aid station in the terminal building to be checked.

At Base Operations I reported to the Navy commander and the Air Force chief ground officer. I was the only Air Force flight surgeon at Guantanamo and the only flight surgeon EASTAF had on site and would begin to organize a party to inspect the wreckage for remains of the aircrew.

Air Force Headquarters was notified of the air crash and an investigating team was ordered from Washington to Guantanamo. They would bring their own flight surgeon to investigate. The air traffic was delayed several hours as planes circled or had to turn back because of low fuel or unsafe landing conditions. By late afternoon, air traffic resumed.

We reported to the helicopter pad and climbed into one of the Navy choppers to over fly the crash site that afternoon. Small explosions continued of the unexploded ammunition. The pilot turned back after a brief look. It was still too dangerous to be at the scene. We had to wait until the next morning before going to the site. Small recurring fires continued into the night.

OCTOBER 24, 1962

The following morning a group of Navy and Air Force men and I hiked up a small barren hill to the north of the runway to look at the crash site. The smoke had cleared and only small pockets of fire were smoldering. "Hell, it's still burning," muttered one of the navy guys. There were only bits of the aircraft left. We elected to go down the hill by vehicle to the crash site. We got out of the Jeeps and could still feel the intense heat. It was so hot on the ground, that despite our heavy leather flying boots we could barely stand in one spot without shifting from foot to foot. We decided to await any further investigation until the Washington team arrived.

We returned to the crash site later in the afternoon. The ground remained hot, twenty-four hours after the crash. The investigating team flight surgeon and I began the difficult task of identifying and removing the remains of the crew. He attempted to photograph the location of the remains and determine the identity of the crew by assigning the remains to the location of the known function of each crew member. Further identification would have to wait until the remains were examined in the States.

Body bags were brought to the site and the remains interred into bags. A couple of dog tags were found that helped separate and identify the remains. "Over here," the other flight surgeon pointed. "Lets start looking for remains over here," he repeated. In a couple of cases the remains were sparse due to the intensity of the fire and resulting explosions. We did the best we could.

The other investigators searched out what was left of the engines, flight controls and other mechanical items for clues to what happened to cause the crash. (In the 1960s there were no black boxes with flight information). There was no evidence of external interference, such as Cuban ground fire. Investigators did not think that the plane was shot down. The only significant sound reported was the change in pitch or whining of the engines, noted by several observers.

When our work was done, the other flight surgeon and I returned to Base Operations where we recorded our initial findings. I was not officially involved in the investigation I was a member of the airlift group and not the investigating team. Fortunately, the squadrons from our base completed their airlifts without incident or significant delays.

In conformity with President Kennedy's speech we successfully "evacuated the dependents and reinforced the American garrison." I thanked my Navy compatriots for their assistance and climbed the crew ladder to board the last Globemaster as it prepared to taxi out to the active runway and depart Guantanamo for the United States. For now, we were just flying home.

A couple of days later we picked up members of the 101st Airborne Division from Fort Campbell, Kentucky. We were prepared for an air invasion of Cuba. We were given our paratroop drop zone maps, and our flight instructions. Our orders were to drop the paratroops, cross the island and if the plane was severely damaged to ditch in the waters south of the island. U.S. Navy destroyers and submarines were patrolling off shore waiting for any eventualities. "They will pick you up," announced the officers in charge. We waited on alert, orders in hand, on a Florida air base runway for an anticipated invasion, should the "Cuban Missile Crisis" not be resolved.

Guantanamo Crash Site

View from the nearby hill

Crash site – Guantanamo Bay, Cuba.

"We returned to the crash site... The ground remained hot
twenty-four hours after the crash..."

Military investigator searches the wreckage.

Investigators diligently search the wreckage for causes of the crash.

BACK HOME

Across the parking lot was my car and beside it stood Millie in a light tan jacket with a blue scarf tied about her blonde hair. She had called Base Ops and gotten the schedule of our return. "Welcome back," she yelled. I stepped out of the operations building into the fresh, chilly, fall air and happily hurried toward the car, climbed in side and we headed for my lake house.

"How was it down there?" Millie asked. "We were all so scared there would be a big war while you were gone." She removed her scarf and tossed her long blonde hair in the breeze of the open window.

After a few moments of silence she glanced toward my side of the car, "Most of the dependents left the base for their families. The base has been on high alert. The news had us all afraid," she said.

"I think it's over," I responded. "Let's go home."

We pulled in the drive to the cottage, lifted my travel bag from the trunk and carried it inside and threw it into my bedroom. I picked up a dry log and some kindling from the wood stack, placed the wood on the andirons of the great fireplace, and started a fire as Millie handed me a cup of steaming hot chocolate. We settled by the hearth as the flames began to slither up the chimney. Outside the sun was setting across the chilled lake. Its dying light reflected gently on the frosty water. "Now, where were we?" she sighed.

"We pulled in the gravel drive to the cottage…We settled by the hearth…
the flames began to slither up the chimney."

SECRET FLIGHT TO ADANA

Unknown to the American public, Premier Khrushchev and President Kennedy, through personal communications and diplomatic channels agreed upon an international compromise. That secret agreement resulted in the United States' removal of what the Russians considered offensive nuclear weapons located in Turkey, near the Russian border.

The Turks, our consistent NATO (North Atlantic Treaty Organization) Cold War ally, were furious over the secret agreement. They felt it would hold them hostage to Soviet movements in or about their borders or territory. Nevertheless, the Soviets announced the voluntary removal of the offending nuclear missiles. Diplomatically, they did not openly relate it to the mutual missile compromise.

The agreement salvaged Khrushchev's reputation, at least for a little while in the Soviet Union after the Cuban Missile Crisis had ended so embarrassingly for him and his government. They removed their missiles from Cuba and we in turn removed ours from Turkey. "We each took our marbles and went home."

Secretary of State, Dean Rusk claimed, "We were eye ball to eye ball and the other person blinked." It seems a true, but trite statement. Perhaps both sides blinked and prevented a disastrous world nuclear conflict.

Kennedy claimed that the missiles in Turkey were obsolete and that removal had been scheduled long before the Cuban Crisis. The Turks remained concerned, but there were other adequate defense arrangements remaining on their territory. As far as I know those particular arrangements were not made public until recently.

The missiles were dismantled with removal of the nuclear warheads. A couple of my squadron's planes secretly flew into Adana, Turkey, and transported the nuclear components back to the United States. Those components were transported in our planes with their own armed military security personnel. There were Army guards, carrying U.S. Army .30 caliber carbines and side arms guarding each missile component on the cross Atlantic flight. The Air Force loadmasters were only allowed to position the containers in the airplane to balance the weight. The loadmasters and air crew had no other contact with the war heads.

While crossing the Atlantic, I climbed down from the crew compartment into the cargo bay of the C-124, looking for a place to sleep, I identified and slept beside the nuclear war head cargo containers. We landed, refueled and crew rested in the Azores. The guards remained with the plane while we crew rested.

After crossing the Atlantic, I was relieved to land safely and watch the nuclear components removed from our planes and secured in big Army trucks, carefully covered by large khaki tarps for their final U.S. destination and cold storage.

"BROKEN ARROW"

The red phone rang. "It's a Broken Arrow exercise," the office corpsman loudly announced. We grabbed our helmets and fatigues and headed to the ambulance station, boarded the trucks and rushed down the dusty road to the airfield. We entered the open gate, acknowledged by the two guards, and drove across the runway into an open adjacent field. There in the field was the carcass of an old transport plane used for fire drills and recovery exercises.

Broken Arrow is the term given to an aircraft incident involving a plane with a nuclear weapon on board, the most feared of aircraft accidents. We hurried to the scene, my men running toting stretchers to assemble to recover the victims. The practice fire had started. The firemen were already there and they and the rescue crew hustled about the old plane hull, now consumed in flames. The decontamination team, dressed in their special protective white suits and hoods scurried around the designated perimeter, their Geiger counters in hand, preparing to isolate nuclear particles and debris that would be present in a real accident.

The practice moved right along, all doing their assigned jobs. In our fatigues with smoke masks in place, we assumed our position to receive the simulated injured at the perimeter of the accident.

The summer temperature and the heat from the fire were overwhelming as we wound up the exercise. I saw that my sweating men had used the smoke masks appropriately and therefore saw no further need for their use. I ordered my corpsmen to remove their masks. "Masks off, men. Put them into the storage bags," I yelled.

All went well, the firemen put out the fire, the injured were triaged by our emergency crew and the hospital team. The referees rushed around with their clipboards checking and grading each units performance.

The following day we met in the Wing Command Office. All senior members of the response teams were represent. The safety officers, grading the exercise presented their findings as successful with only a few significant suggestions.

Without any apparent or prior concern the fire chief rose and very critically pointed out that the flight surgeon's office and the hospital triage team had removed their masks before the exercise was complete.

I couldn't believe his remarks and I rose to defend our decision. "Colonel." I said to the wing commander, "It was so hot I thought it unnecessary to risk heat exhaustion once our tasks were performed and I ordered the removal of the masks."

The Colonel glanced at the fire chief and said nothing. I further commented, "Sir, I didn't even see the firemen with their masks in use at all."

The chief seemed perturbed at my comments. He rose again and indignantly explained, "Yes, that's right. We don't have them, but they are on order."

I couldn't believe the comments. Yet, to the assembled group he had made his point. "Sir," I added, "what if it had been a real Broken Arrow?"

There was no answer. In the military, if it's on order, it must be okay, I wondered.

"HAPPY THANKSGIVING – EAT YOUR SPAM."
NOVEMBER 1962

It was summer in the Southern Hemisphere where the seasons are reversed from the Northern Hemisphere. I was, barely south of the equator that November. I got there by some ridiculous miscommunication.

At a morning briefing, my commander had asked, "Who would like to conga?" I was in the back of the conference room not paying attention (Those were usually boring gatherings) and I thought he was speaking of the up and coming holiday officer's dance. Well, I thought. I barely know how to waltz so maybe I could learn to conga. No one volunteered so leaned back in my chair and I daringly raised my hand. "Good," he said, "you can go."

"Oh, go where?" I answered, obviously confused.

"To the Congo," he said.

"Oh my, the Congo?" I responded. I had already gone once. The Air Force was still providing the UN air support to carry equipment, arms, and ammunition throughout the African region, during the 1960s war in the former Belgian Congo. Well, I thought, I'll just assign someone else from the flight surgeon's office who hasn't been to Congo.

After reviewing the staff list I decided, yes, Peter Townsend is the one. I picked up the phone and dialed his home number. Peter was one of my favorite doctors in our flight surgeon's office.

He answered, "Yes, this is Captain Townsend, what can I do for you?"

"Peter," I said, "it's your time, I've looked on the schedule board and its your time to go on an overseas mission."

"I can't," he firmly answered. "My little girl has a fever."

"Well, how high is it?" I asked.

"A hundred and four," he said.

"Have you given her aspirin? Have you iced her down?" I asked. (Aspirin is now rarely used to lower children's fever).

"I've done all that…. She has a bad cough and I've started her on penicillin. I'm not going. My wife will leave me if I leave."

"Peter, you have to go, it's your turn in the rotation," I said.

"Not going, court martial me if you have to," he defiantly answered.

Hell, Peter, you know that no one's going to court martial you. I'll call Major Perry and see what we can do, see if we can find someone else."

The major, administrative officer, answered the phone, "Says he won't go huh, does he?"

"Yes, sir, he said that," I answered.

Major Perry hesitated for a moment, "Well, we've got someone else to go."

"Who?" I answered.

Without hesitation he said, "You, you're single. You have no children. You can go instead."

"Yes, but I've already been once."

There was a pause, then "Yes, but you're single," he repeated.

Before I knew it I was back in Congo in an isolated area with landing gear trouble, awaiting spare parts from the outside world.

Back in the States my squadron was having a dance and turkey dinner. I was stuck with a sick plane, an unhappy crew, and almost no food. Six or eight bored airmen with no place to go is no darn fun.

"Who knows how to cook?" I asked.

"Sergeant Montalvo can cook," one of the airmen quickly responded.

"It's Thanksgiving season and what's for dinner?" one of the pilots cheerfully and wishfully asked.

Sergeant Montalvo answered, "Sorry, we don't have any turkey, but we do have spam. We can't drink the water, but we do have beer." He glanced over at a huge sack labeled in English, Arkansas Rice, "I swapped some beer for that sack of Arkansas rice from the UN troops and I've got some vegetables from the locals. I'm boiling the water and washing the vegetables and I'm making Thanksgiving dinner," he boasted.

A younger airman, not to be left out, stood beside him and proudly commented, "He means we're both fixing something to eat."

Spam, rice, vegetables, and Heinekens doesn't seem like home at Thanksgiving season, but on a damn hot and thirsty day in Congo, with beer to boot, who's complaining?

POST THANKSGIVING
BACK TO LEO

Our crew received the parts for our sick airplane, jacked up the wheel and wing, repaired the landing gear, and left Elisabethville to return to the airfield at Leopoldville. Our plane pulled up to the hanger at Leo's N'Djili Aeroport. The plane from Elisabethville required more extensive maintenance at Leopoldville before it could be flown back to Europe and the States.

I reported to the command office for a flight out of Congo. Since my squadron's mission was nearly complete and our plane was delayed days by mechanical problems, I needed to be back in the States. I would likely go ahead of the squadron.

The ONUC in Congo, the United Nation Forces (Forces de L'Organisation des Unis Du Congo) were made up of multinationals. Each country's troops had a specific area of responsibility. It was comparable to the "Tower of Babel" with all different languages. French and English were the two most common languages. French was spoken in the old Belgian Congo and English was preferred with the UN forces.

In Leopoldville the Norwegians controlled the airfield and air port terminal and the Swedish government's personnel provided the air combat pilots and ground maintenance for the Saab jets (SAAB J-29s), that flew in the minimal air combat over the Congo. A rebel airplane would occasionally fly over, drop a few benign, ineffective bombs and have to be chased away.

The Indian and Pakistani medical units rendered the medical care in the UN Hospital in Leopoldville. A small contingency of Malaysian troops also participated. There were a few dispensaries in the towns of Albertville, Elisabethville and I believe Stanleyville, Congo.

The Italians supplied a small number of medical support troops.

The Canadians and the Free Irish handled communications along with the Nigerians who also provided the limited security in Congo.

The local or National Army of the Congo was distributed throughout the region as they fought against the seceding sections of the country, i.e., the rebels of Katanga Province and a number of Belgian and other European white mercenaries.

The United States Air Force provided the airlift transport of men, fuel, ammunition, armored vehicles, and the transport of antiaircraft guns for the UN Forces. One of our earlier flights, brought the Vice Air Marshall of Sweden from Stockholm to Congo to command the UN Air Forces.

At the N'Djili Aeroport, our living quarters were prefab units, air-conditioned and located in an isolated area of the huge hanger, separated by temporary walls from the rest of the building. There the rotating aircrews slept, day or night between flights.

At three a.m. local time, a staff sergeant awakened me from a deep sleep. "Doc," he said as he flashed his hand light in my face and gently shook me awake, "they need you over at the air terminal."

"What? They what?" I mumbled as I attempted to awaken.

"The Norwegian troops need you over at the terminal. They have a man they think is having a heart attack."

"One of our men?" I hastily asked.

"No, sir, some Belgian or French guy," he answered. "I think he's a civilian."

"Hell, we don't treat civilians," I protested.

"Yes, sir, I know, "I told them, but they want you anyway."

I dressed rapidly and rushed over to the terminal with my corpsman in the UN Jeep.

Inside, a large crowd of frantic, agitated, Congolese civilians and several members of the Congolese Army were pushing and shoving at each other. The soldiers were trying to control the unruly crowd inside and outside the terminal.

The local native Congolese protestors, inside the terminal wanted to climb over the ticket counters to get to the man who allegedly stole huge sums of money from the Congolese government. They told me he was trying to escape the Congo on a Sabena airplane, scheduled to arrive that morning at the air field.

Sabena Airways was able to maintain a limited international flight schedule into and out of the Congo despite the civil war. Sabena airlifts were used to evacuate the Europeans, especially the whites, from the old Belgian Congo during the earlier months of conflict and during the rough days of initial separation of the Congo from Belgian domination.

Through a side door I was ushered into the back room of the terminal ticket office by the Norwegian, Lieutenant Danielsen whom I had met earlier.

On a military stretcher was a heavy set, ruddy-faced man, sweating profusely, having trouble getting his breath, coughing and complaining bitterly of chest pain. He was obviously frightened by the restless natives and police.

I hurried to him, loosened his shirt, listened to his chest and checked his blood pressure. His heart was racing; a number that I could not count and his blood systolic pressure was well over 200 mm of mercury. I guessed he was in atrial fibrillation and acute heart failure. I found a vein in his forearm and started him on intravenous fluids that I had brought in my medical bag. I gave him morphine I.V. to calm him and attempt to slow his heart rate. I was afraid to give him anything else before getting an EKG. I gave him nitroglycerine for his chest pain then announced to the lieutenant and to a Congolese police officer near by, "We needed to get this man down town to the UN Hospital, right now."

The Congolese police officer resisted moving him to the hospital. He wanted to take him to jail. The problem was to get away from the crowd outside the ticket office. The officer spoke no English, so I had to do the best I could with the bits of French I could remember.

Within a half hour I convinced the policeman that if this man died they would never find the money they claimed he had stolen, some three hundred thousand dollars equivalent in Belgian and Congolese currency. He argued his point but eventually agreed, but said, translated by the Norwegian, "I must ride with you to the UN Hospital." (That was a good idea and if the fellow could survive the police could question him safely at the UN Hospital).

Now we had to escape the violent crowd. The lieutenant had a UN Volkswagen bus with only three of four gears working. He had one weapon, a German Lugar pistol to defend against the rowdy crowd should we need it. We slipped out a side door as Congolese troops confronted the angry crowd in the war scarred terminal lobby.

Soon as the crowd discovered that we had left the building and we were headed off in our VW bus they emptied the terminal, destroyed windows and what furniture remained in the shot up building. We were lucky to be out on the dirt and gravel road headed toward the main paved highway into town. At four a.m. the darkness was our best defense.

"Look at behind us," the lieutenant said in his best English as he drove the vehicle onto the main road to town. Several sets of auto lights were gaining on us. We were going as fast as we could in our best third gear.

"Stay in the middle of the road," I yelled to him. "That might keep the cars from coming along side." We had no idea what the people chasing us had beside the sticks we had seen in the terminal.

We remained in the middle of the road, yet a car with the locals hanging out the windows with big sticks in their hands pulled along our right side, half on and half off the road. They were throwing their sticks and reaching out at our vehicle with their arms and hands and throwing rocks at us.

The lieutenant drove and one of us (I don't remember who) held the sole pistol out the window and pointed the gun toward the driver. Fear gripped his dark eyes. He swerved to the right and crashed off the road down a shallow dirt embankment. All we could see were head lights shining in every direction. We surmised that the car was turning over. We feared to stop to find out what had happened. *

The cars behind us stopped at the wreck site. We drove into Leopoldville, still in third gear, to the UN Hospital. Those in pursuit may have thought the wrecked car was our vehicle. The guard at the gate stopped us, but after checking our military passports allowed us, in the marked UN vehicle to enter the hospital grounds. A couple of uniformed medics met us and rushed the Belgian guy into the hospital. We turned him over to the Indian and Pakistani doctors.

Dr. El Khory and Dr. Sighn, the physicians in charge, assured us that he would be safe. They kept a Congolese policeman as well as a uniformed military guard outside his room, both to keep him from escaping and to protect him.

The sun was rising above the horizon on a new day in Congo. We conversed briefly with the doctors, left the Congolese police officer with them and headed back to the airfield. We drove down the same dusty road to the airfield. We looked for the wrecked car but did not see it. We never knew what happened when the car ran off the road. It remained a mystery.

A couple of days later, I returned during day light to the UN Hospital. The patient was improving. The police had questioned him, yet no charges had been made against him. My sergeant, a medic, and I were invited to stay for tea. "Sorry, but we must get back to the airfield," I said to the staff.

Going out, my sergeant turned to me and quietly whispered, "You have just insulted them by refusing tea."

We turned around in our tracks and hurried back up the concrete steps into the hospital, just for tea. Each afternoon, thereafter we joined our Indian and Pakistani medical friends for tea or coffee. We set up canvas safari chairs and a table on the airfield tarmac beside the antiaircraft guns and our make shift medical tents and invited our friends from the UN hospital. From then on we took regular "afternoon tea."

*We were advised at the embassy that if for any reason we were involved in a traffic accident that we were to leave the scene and get to the embassy immediately. There we would be safe. We were told that any European involved in an accident would be considered guilty and well may be beaten with sticks or stones by the locals. Justice would be meted out at the accident scene. The embassy staff could sort it all out if we returned to the embassy's diplomatic protection

"We took regular afternoon tea"

UN Hospital – Dr. El Khori and author, Leopoldville

Flight Line dispensary – Congo 1962-1963

Nearby we set up primitive accommodations for
afternoon tea with our UN medical friends.

LEAVING CONGO

We completed our mission. I finished the second tour of duty in the former Belgian Congo and I was headed back to Europe and the States. The "New Tape Operation" was the first successful major airlift for the big C-133's of the 1st Air Transport Squadron of MATS. This airplane carried a much greater payload than the C-124s that had previously been used in Congo. The C-133 was designed initially to carry the Atlas and Titan intercontinental missiles.

Base Ops at N'Djili issued orders for me to fly back to Rhein Main or Chatereaux or Evereaux, which ever had a flight headed in that direction. Dispersed there were units of the 31st Squadron and 15th Squadron TDY (temporary duty). The orders directed the most current available transportation. The orders read, "To depart by a certain time and date allowing appropriate and expedient travel time."

I approached Colonel Jones, a straight-laced officer about traveling on one of his planes north. When he saw that I had grown a scruffy beard while out in the bush on our shuttle flights he commented, "Not with that shaggy beard, Doc. No one in my squadron has a beard."

He was a tall, lean, clean-shaven guy with a short crew cut of his already thinning hair. He was a real "spit and polish" officer. His khaki clothes were perfectly pressed, even in the sweltering heat of the Congo. He was a professional.

Off went the beard. I flew in one of his C-133s to Kano, Nigeria and then to Tripoli in Libya. There I hopped one of the C-130s going over the Mediterranean and the Alps to Germany.

When the craft landed near Frankfurt, I hitched a ride in a little Opal with a German officer, Lieutenant Klingmann. He was in Libya for joint tactical bombing practice exercises with the Americans and NATO (North Atlantic Treaty Organization). I was surprised when we cleared the ice and snow from the lieutenant's car that had been parked outside in the cold German winter that within a few minutes the officer managed to start the little Opal with no difficulty.

At our home base, I spent more time with Col. Jones when a C-133 from his squadron, "The First," mysteriously disappeared over the Atlantic Ocean. Parts of the plane were discovered floating on the ocean surface by a commercial German freighter, including the flight jacket of one of the flight engineers with his name inscribed on the jacket. The remnants of the plane, collected from the ocean were sent to our base. In one of our huge hangers the aircraft manufacture's civilian engineers attempted to reconstruct and determine the plane's impact on the ocean's surface.

It was my job as flight surgeon to accompany Col. Jones when he visited each of the crew's families to notify them of the loss of their husbands. It was a terrible experience delivering such messages, especially to young wives with little children.

As a surgery resident before the service, I had often informed families of tragic incidents, but these men were friends or fellow airmen with whom I had flown, some of whom I had shared drinks at the bar. This was different, yet Col. Jones was a tough soldier and though inside I'm sure he was distressed, he never showed any emotion with the families. "This is our job," he affirmed to me as we left one house. "This is what airmen do. We fly and some of us die. That's just the way it is," he unapologetically declared. He was the same officer who responded to my suggestion for a medal for one of my corpsmen in Africa, "I don't give medals, I give promotions."

I was asked to participate with the Aircraft Accident Investigation Board. Though denied by some, because of mechanical problems, the C-133 was later taken out of the Air Force inventory. It was replaced by the huge Lockheed C-5A.

This accident investigation required that the medical records of each crew man be immediately removed from the files to avoid any possible tampering with the records. Each record would be studied for psychological elements as well as general physical problems that might have bearing on the flight. It seemed to me that the investigating teams always wanted to blame pilot error. It was much easier than confronting the manufacturer or the maintenance sections of the military.

We viewed the mock up of the lost aircraft in the hanger, and examined the recovered pieces of the plane and the flight engineers intact flying jacket. While studying the remnants I remembered that we lost an engine with a propeller control problem over the Sahara Desert en route to the Congo. It was necessary to return to Libya for maintenance and repair of the engine before we continued to the Congo. I wondered if the missing plane had similar engine trouble, but I never knew.

Contract Sabena aircraft carried Congolese and UN soldiers about the Congo.

USAF C-133 (New Tape Operation) on the ground.

Isolated guard gate at the air field, probably Elisabethville, Congo.

GROUNDED

Winter 1962 - 1963

On a bitter, icy winter's day in Dover I could see through the morning haze ice skaters on the small frozen lake just down our shallow hill. I noticed particularly the young ice skaters already racing about that early morning. There was one fellow that was taller and appeared older than the little kids. He seemed to be skating about with no particular direction, yet fairly near our small dock that extended out into the lake. I turned from the window to start a fire in our stone fireplace to break the chill in our cottage.

When I again looked out there were a couple of older looking skaters in heavier coats gathered at the end of our dock by the hazy, single, light at the dock's edge. They appeared to be talking. They looked toward our house for a few moments and then skated away. One of the skaters remained and sat down on the end of the dock. He looked like he was fixing or taking off his skates. I moved from the window to the kitchen to start the coffee and returned to the living room to stoke the now glowing fire, already warming the room.

A few minutes later while dressing for the day I heard a soft knock on the kitchen door. We rarely used the front door. Usually the knocks on our door were loud, but this was an unsure irregular knock. I wondered if some kid was at the door. A few kids lived in the neighborhood and were always selling something. I yelled out, "Just a minute, I'll be there."

When I opened the door a tall guy, one of the pilots from my fighter squadron, was standing at the door holding ice skates in his gloved hand. This perhaps was the fellow I saw at the end of our dock a few minutes before. "Hi, Doc," he said, "may I come in?"

"Sure," I said, "come in. Take off your jacket and come in by the fire and warm up."

He kicked the snow from his shoes on the doormat, removed his jacket and scarf, came through the kitchen into the living room to the blazing fire and began warming his hands.

"Cold out there, huh?" I said to him.

"Yeah, pretty cold," he answered. "Doc, I know its early and I really should come to the office, but I need to talk to you."

"Its okay. I'm up and it's good to have company. The rest of the guys are out on flights and it's lonesome in the house, glad you came over," I said. "Would you like some coffee or hot chocolate? I'm just getting the coffee and stuff going for the day."

He moved away from the fire and sat down in a nearby over stuffed chair. "Yeah, the chocolate sounds best," he said.

We both decided to have chocolate, rather than coffee. We had seen each other at the officers club party the night before but had no conversation. This morning we were both recovering from the party.

"What can I do for you?" (I shall call him John, though that was not his name).

It's about flying," he said.

"Flying, what about flying?" I asked.

"I can't fly the bird any more," he said.

"You mean the 101 or the T-33?" I asked, now somewhat confused.

"The 101 bird!" he abruptly answered. "I just can't fly it any more, I go to pieces when I start my roll out. I'm always afraid something's going wrong. I don't know what's happened to me. I just can't fly it any more. I panic when the "horn" goes off."

I knew that the McDonnell F-101B Voodoo, a twin engine jet fighter aircraft, was known to have "pitch up" problems with certain "potential stalls and attitudes" of the plane resulting in "flat spin" and loss of control of the plane.

The horn was a warning signal, that sounded when the plane was approaching an unsafe attitude or "angle of attack." If the pilot did not respond to the "horn" an automatic control took over and pushed the nose over into a more stable attitude. It is loud and scary to hear the horn. All pilots complained about the horn's sudden noise. If a "flat spin" and loss

119

of control occurred under a certain low altitude, there was a mandatory ejection of the pilot and navigator / radar observer because there was no time to recover the plane.

"John, you know you are a damn good pilot. I have flown with you, both day and night, and I have every confidence in your ability," I said. "My first night flight was with you."

"Yeah, but you've only flown with me in the T-33" (An older and more stable single jet trainer), he said.

"Okay, but I'll fly with you in a 101, if you'd like to see what the problem is." I answered. "Hell, I trust my life with you, you know that. We can go up to the higher altitude and test the horn together. Have you talked to Colonel Crain about this?"

"No, I thought I'd come to see you first, you're the flight surgeon. Maybe you could ground me for a while and I can think about it," he said.

His temporary solution may seem reasonable to him, but to me it seemed more complicated. I was always concerned, maybe superstitiously, that some fears were premonitions of a dreadful future event.

"Well, we'll have to talk to Colonel Crain (squadron commander) together and see what he thinks. I know he doesn't want to lose a good pilot like you from the squadron." I thought about what John had said. I had never come across this problem before in any of my aircrews. "How long has this been going on?" I asked.

"Several months, since before you came to the squadron, even before last year's loss of the 101 over the Atlantic," he said.

I asked, "Nobody knows what happened to that plane, do they?"

"No, the accident board never figured it out. Those guys just disappeared. No radio contact or warning or any thing, they just disappeared off the radar. They never even found any wreckage or debris."

"Is that what has got you upset?" I asked.

"Must be," he said. "I look down and see that cold water and fear every unusual noise in the cockpit when I am flying. I'm just waiting for something to happen. Last week my RO (radar observer) asked me what was wrong when we landed. I told him, that I didn't feel good and was going to the flight surgeon's office. I claimed that I had a sinus problem and a headache, but I didn't go till now."

"John, you've done the right thing coming here today. I'm going to call the squadron ops officer and put you on DNIF (duty not involving flying) because you sound a little "stuffed up" to me. Yes, I think you should be medically grounded till we work this out. We can talk to Colonel Crain tomorrow and see where we go." I said. "This grounding will not affect your flying record. Officially it's medical. Have some more hot chocolate and we'll try to work this problem out,"

"Yeah," He said and sipped his steaming chocolate as we silently looked out at the new fresh, lovely, falling snow.

I called the squadron commander the next day and asked him if I could meet with him privately, that I wished to discuss a flying situation which I felt was of vital importance to a member of the squadron. I didn't name the officer, nor did I advise him that I had grounded the individual. I could explain that later. He agreed and asked that I come over to his office at squadron headquarters after the morning flight briefing. That was fine. I arranged to meet with him.

In his office, the commander reminded me and further explained to me that Air Force Regulations stated that a pilot must be ready and available to fly any airplane in the inventory that he was trained and currently qualified to fly. There were no exceptions. He must be prepared to fly or consider resigning his commission. That was a tough rule, but the military could not allow picking and choosing arbitrarily by the pilots. That would put too much restraint on the missions required by each unit.

"It is that simple," explained Colonel Crain. "For now we can counsel the involved pilot and seek to remedy the problem."

"Refusing to fly an airplane because of "fear of flying," is a court martial offense," he reaffirmed. "That would be up to a Flying Board to handle such a situation." He made it clear that he did not want to lose a good pilot and that together we would try to work out the problem.

Crain treated his men as if each was his own son. He was firm and an excellent commander. He was a seasoned pilot. He flew fighters in the China-Burma-India theater of the Second World War. He knew his men and he knew his mission.

John and I met with the squadron commander and discussed the problem. The commander listened sympathetically yet reaffirmed the fact that eventually John would have to return to flying the Voodoo F-101 as the primary operational aircraft in the squadron. We all agreed on a temporary grounding, and that I would record it on his record as an upper respiratory problem. He would be placed on ground control duty dealing with administrative matters for a while.

I suggested a psychological consult at Philadelphia Naval Hospital or Walter Reed Army Hospital, to see if some insight might be brought into the situation. (I was the psych officer on paper in the flight surgeon's office. I had little to no psychology or psychiatric experience, only two years of surgery training, and I hated psych stuff).

I said to Col. Crain, "I want a real psychologist or psychiatrist to consult. I'm too close to the squadron and its men to be objective." He agreed.

No one flying wanted a psych consult on his or her medical record. It was a macho or ego thing. I saw no alternative and thought that talking honestly to someone off our base would free the individual from the pressure surrounding his work. Surprisingly, John agreed to go for the consult.

To keep his flying status and not lose his flying pay because of the temporary grounding, I agreed, after I okayed his return to limited flying duty to fly with John in the T-33 on pick ups and other limited flights. We flew in the T-33 with no problems. I think we both enjoyed the flights.
We discussed with the commander flying in the 101. I reaffirmed my confidence in John's capability and told him I would fly regular pick up flights in the 101 or I would be willing to fly the high altitude flights with the partial pressure suits and test the Horn. (It was unlikely that we would have to eject at the higher altitudes since there was ample opportunity to correct the possibility of the so-called flat spin). John was still not willing to try it.

The commander did all that he could to help John resolve that fear, short of a court martial. Some times the fear, real and unreal, is so great that it is not correctable. When the string ran out of the many options to keep John flying in the Air Force he resigned his commission rather than go before a court martial board. The Air Force lost an excellent pilot.

Perhaps John was right, there was something wrong with that airplane. A few months after his resignation from the Air Force, the squadron mysteriously lost another plane over the Atlantic waters, the same icy waters John had feared. It was the same story, no trace of the F-101 or crew was ever found. It simply "disappeared off the radar." Both of the crew members were my friends. Together, we were fitted for our altitude pressure suits.

Grounded

"Out my window on a bitter, icy winter's day in Dover I could see through the morning haze, ice skaters on the small frozen lake ..."

A CASE OF WHAT

The corpsman strolled into my office. "Sir, the airman in the waiting room says he wants to talk to you rather than the office corpsmen."

"Sure, I'll see him. Put him in room four."

I knocked on the door and gradually opened it. The airman looked to be about nineteen, twenty at most. He sat quietly on the exam table. "You wanted to talk to me?" I asked.

"Yes, sir. It's kind of a personal matter," he said, dropping his head, first glancing at the floor then directly at me.

"Okay, what's the problem?"

He was fidgety, glanced around the room then concentrated his eyes toward the ceiling and quietly mumbled, "Sir, I think I've picked up something."

I knew what he meant and it wasn't lifting. "Where do you think you picked it up?"

"Think it was in Congo or Chatereaux."

"Did you go by Jimmies Place in Chatereaux?"

He again glanced down at the floor. "Yes, sir, I did."

"When did you get back?" I asked.

"A couple of days ago."

"What are your symptoms?"

"Stinging and burning and a little yellow discharge," he confessed with a shaking of his head in disbelief.

"Have you been home yet?"

"Yes, sir, but I told my wife I was just too tired."

I knew what he was saying.

He squirmed a bit on the exam table, "Sir, I tried to confess to my wife."

"What did you say?"

"Well, I told her right out that I was sorry, but I had brought home a case of the clap."

"What did she say?"

"Sir," he paused, "she didn't understand." He grinned. "She said, 'that's okay, 'cause I'm tired of those cases of Madiera that you usually bring home from Spain.'"

I stepped out of the room. "Sergeant, get us a urine specimen from this airman and wait for the lab report and notify me of the results, then we'll likely start him on his Penicillin regime."

NEW YEAR'S EVE IN LONDON, OOPS, BOSTON

It was all planned. Our aircraft commander selected his crew. We were all young. We all wanted to go to London for New Year's Eve. It was settled. Yes, our schedule could take us to Mildenhall and we would arrive conveniently too late to be unloaded on New Year's Eve and would lay over for a few days in England. "Good planning," I said to my friend. He invited me to go along as the squadron's flight surgeon.

Since the married guys wanted to be home for New Years celebrations with their families, it was easy to assemble a few bachelors from the squadron to celebrate in London.

All we had to do was to persuade the scheduling officer to set up the trip. "Yes, we have a trip to Mildenhall and Rhein Main," he told our aircraft commander. "We were going to hold it till after New Year's Day."

"Oh, we'll take it and will go earlier," our aircraft commander volunteered. "I'll find some of the unmarried guys to go."

"Okay," said the scheduler. "If you can get a volunteer crew we can schedule it. We really need to send this priority cargo out and the colonel will be pleased if it is not delayed 'till after New Years."

With that done, the plane was loaded and ready the next day. "We'll add fuel at Goose Bay (Labrador) and refuel at Lajes (Azores) and crew rest there. If we have a tail wind, we can make Mildenhall by New Year's Eve," said the copilot as he explained the conjured plan to me.

I never realized that the schedule could be shuffled around so easily. I thought the schedules were rigid, but when the young, highly motivated male element is added, almost any thing is possible in the military.

It was early morning, December 29 when we reported to Base Ops for our pre flight instructions, weather update and confirmation of our flight plan. "Looks good," said the pilot to the crew as we climbed aboard the huge Globemaster in the morning haze. The sun was rising on a dreary cold day, but a day we hoped would be enjoyable. We had just the right crew to carry out our mission and perhaps a bit of fun on the side.

With the preflight accomplished, we started our rumbling movement onto the active runway and were soon airborne into the low, hazy clouds, headed northeast toward Labrador. The second flight engineer was making coffee and passing it out as we settled into our flight along the Atlantic coast.

"We'll stay along the coast and you can see New York in the distance out the port windows if it is not too cloudy," the A/C said. "Come on up to the cockpit and you can see better from the instructor seat." (The instructor seat is a little seat between and slightly aft of the pilots so the flight instructor or flight examiner can watch the instruments and observe the actions of the pilot and copilot in flight).

Soon we were in the New York sector at about eight or nine thousand feet as we looked out at an overcast sky.

"This is the sector we fly in the 98th (Air Defense Squadron) on practice intercepts," I mentioned to the pilot and copilot. "We get darn close to Yankee Stadium. You can't see the pitching or base runners, but you can see the lights of the stadium. Its really neat to see the New York lights, especially at night."

We droned on through the New York sector on autopilot and as we settled back to relax, the engineer noticed that the oil pressure on engine number two (port inboard) was slowly dropping.

(I later began to think I was bad luck since I had been on several flights with engine problems). "Not so," said one officer. "These old planes are just worn out and need much tender care."

"Lieutenant," the flight engineer said to the A/C, "I'm having trouble keeping the oil pressure up on number two and the temp's rising. It's overheating."

"How long has this been going on?" the A/C responded and turned toward the engineer to see if he, from the left seat could see the temperature gage on the engineer's panel.

(Many gages are duplicated on the plane and crew members can read the gages from several positions. The pilots and engineers particularly share some common instruments and controls).

"About fifteen minutes, but I thought I could adjust the fuel mixture and it might get better, but it hasn't," the flight engineer answered.

The A/C asked the navigator, "Exactly where are we?"

"We're just out of the New York sector, according to the radar, just over the coast," said the navigator.

"What do you think, chief? Do you think we'll have to shut it down?" the A/C asked in a concerned voice.

"Sir, I think we better shut 'er down if the temp keeps going up," the engineer answered, now appearing agitated, busily tapping gauges to be sure each was correct, and moving panel control handles and knobs.

Meanwhile the copilot pulled out the charts and landing plates and looked for a place to go down if we had to make an emergency landing. He leaned over from his right seat and showed the A/C the map and chart that showed a base in New Hampshire. "Looks like Pease is the nearest military base where we can land and get maintenance," he said.

"How is the engine now," the A/C asked the engineer?

"No better, sir, still heating up," the engineer answered, now seemingly alarmed. I could see sweat on his forehead as he wiped his brow with his sleeve.

"Let's start the shutdown and feather the prop," ordered the pilot. "Number two, everybody, number two."

"Roger, I'm starting," said the engineer as he began to shut off the fuel to number two engine at his control panel. He seemed relieved that the decision had been made to go ahead and shut the engine down.

"Roger, number two," responded the copilot. He switched the radio controls and contacted ground control for instructions and permission to be directed to Pease Air Base. He identified our plane by tail number and advised the operator that we were shutting down and feathering one engine and would need help in directions to Pease Air Base.

"We've got you on radar," answered a ground controller. He gave the copilot directions and heading toward Pease. "We see you clearly and can lead you into Pease airspace. We'll notify the tower that you will be making an emergency landing on three engines."

"Roger," said the copilot. "We understand. We'll maintain contact."

I had only been in a plane once or twice before, while on a mission flight, that had to shut down an engine, but this was standard procedure and the crew carried out their duties flawlessly. "Doc, don't worry we do this all the time for practice on our check rides. No problem. Sometimes we shut down two engines, but not with a full load as we have today," said the aircraft commander.

I had flown a few "around the pole base check rides" when the examiner pilot ordered the examined pilot to shut down more than one engine.

I looked out the port window and noticed only a thin stream of whitish smoke trailing from engine number two, the inboard engine, as the propeller began to slow its spin.

"It's feathered and it won't cause much drag," said the pilot, as I twisted to see out the window.

"Flaps set and gear down," affirmed the copilot to the A/C as we approached the runway. "Looks like they've got the fire trucks out," he said into his mike.

The landing was smooth and the control tower directed us to a parking spot by a huge gray maintenance hanger. "Shut 'em down," the A/C said to the copilot and engineer.

The fire trucks surrounded the plane and the base firemen scurried to the port side of the plane. The engine had stopped smoking. There was no further danger of fire.

"We'll watch that engine for a while," the fire chief yelled from the port side up to the cockpit. The A/C slipped the cockpit glass open and leaned out to wave an acknowledgement to the fire crew.

The flight crew checked the instruments and completed their post-landing checklist. We climbed down from the belly of the plane and huddled in the freezing, gently falling snow, looking at the engine and talking to the fire chief and the ground crew. "Looks like you boys will be here a while," said the maintenance sergeant.

The ground crew rolled a huge canvas tent like structure and enclosed the engine for protection from the cold. The maintenance crew would work inside the protective screen on the engine. The sergeant took the A/C aside, "Sir, you may need an engine change from the looks of that engine. Yep, your crew may be here a few days, it being New Years and all."

The A/C returned to where were standing and announced, "Sorry guys, we won't make London. Maybe next year."

My friend, Lt. Rogers, one of the two navigators, chimed in. "Boston is not far and I have a girlfriend in the stage musical, My Fair Lady that's playing in Boston. I'll bet she can get us dates with the cast."

"Boston it is." responded our aircraft commander with a big smile. "Happy New Year, Boston!"

Less than forty-eight hours after settling into the transient officers quarters several of us rode a bus into Boston and stood by the stage door of My Fair Lady waiting for our promised dates. It was to be a memorable New Year's Eve in Boston.

"New Year's Eve in London, Oops, Boston."

"We climbed down the crew ladder and huddled in the freezing ... snow."

"… in the freezing snow looking at the engine …
"Looks like you boys will be here a while," said the maintenance sergeant.

Note: Engine #2's (port inboard) prop does not appear feathered.

FOGGY NIGHT TO BERLIN

During a freezing late January and early February in 1963 I was in Frankfurt, Germany. I contacted my former fiancée. We had dinner at a friend's house, a doctor at the 97th Army Hospital where my former fiancée worked as a civilian contract nurse. A subsequent date was canceled when I received orders at the BOQ to report to Operations Headquarters at nearby Rhein Main Airfield.

The fog was so thick that I knew nothing was flying. I wondered why I had been summoned. "You're to report in flight suit with cold weather clothes for a few days," the sergeant advised when he opened the door of the staff car that would take me to the air field.

"I've been in hot climate and don't have any cold weather clothes." I answered.

"Maybe someone at Ops will lend you a jacket," he volunteered.

He carried printed orders that read, " ... to observe stress on flight crews during flight exercise," whatever that meant. "I don't know where you are going," he said. "All I know is that I'm to bring you to Base Ops."

After a briefing at Base Operations – No jackets were available so I wore extra clothes under my flying togs. I rode out to a huge and barely visible Globemaster sitting on the edge of the runway. The crew was on board. "We can't fly in all this fog, can we?" I asked the loadmaster as he helped me with my travel bag up the crew ladder into the cargo compartment.

"What in the world is all this equipment," I asked as I entered the cargo interior of the plane. I looked around and all sort of electronic stuff surrounded us.

There were two lieutenant colonels, and two extra navigators as well as the full compliment of crew members. Why is all this brass here?

I wondered. This plane was from the 15th Squadron, not my regular squadron. I wondered why I was even here? My orders were from EASTAF, our mutual Command that had authority to send me wherever they pleased.

"Doc, You're assigned to us since you are the only 1607th flight surgeon in Germany right now," said one of the officers standing by the electrical equipment. One of our squadrons was on temporary duty at Chatereaux where this plane had been especially equipped for tonight's mission. "We've been waiting for a night like this for our mission," added the officer.

For weeks the East Germans and Russian military blocked the railroads and highways from West Germany along the ground corridors into West Berlin. They were cutting off the food shipments, coal, fuel, and heating oil from West Germany in an attempt to starve and freeze the West Berliners in midwinter. They intended that East Germany take over and occupy all of Berlin. *

"They are also jamming our radar and harassing our flights into Berlin," said one of the navigators. "We're going to fly into Berlin to test their radar jamming system."

"In this fog?" I asked aloud. "Can we get into Berlin in all this?"

"Yes, this is the perfect time," he said. "There is absolutely no aircraft traffic over Germany because of the bad weather. We'll be the lone flight into the Berlin corridors tonight. They'll pick us up on their radar and they'll try to jam us and we'll persist in our landings. They will know we have a new and secret navigation system."

"Wow!" I said, and again I asked, "What's all this electronic stuff?"

"This electronic and monitoring equipment is what we couldn't tell you about for the last couple of months. This is where your navigator pals have been at night, learning this new navigation system." He explained. "This is damn top-secret stuff."

The engines began their whining and their sputtering roar. The blue exhaust flames lighted up the fog around the engines. There was an eerie, bright, mystic haze, shadows, and crystal glares of bouncing light about each engine as the propellers turned. We taxied out, slowly moved toward the runway following a ground direction truck. We prepared to take off into the soupy fog, that horrible night.

The lights in the cockpit reflected the glare of the outside fog as if we were inside a bright snow bank. Even the runway lights were hard to see. The pilot switched to low red interior lights to protect our vision. "See, we've got a lead truck guiding us out to the active runway," said the navigator. We could see only the hazy glare of the circulating light on the truck's roof. "We'll just follow the haze to the runway then we'll depend on our instruments."

I held my breath as we rumbled down the runway. We were soon airborne into the dark night headed toward Templehoff Air Field in Berlin. Parts of the runway at Templehoff had housing developments almost up to the edge of the runways. The landing corridor was narrow. There were three Allied landing corridors into West Berlin. One of the corridors was for British, another for French and the third for Americans planes since the three Western Allies occupied West Berlin. The Soviets occupied East Berlin. They had a separate airfield in the Eastern sector of the city.

The weather remained terrible as we approached Berlin in a dense fog. At first we could fly above the fog and clouds, but as we approached the city our plane descended to a lower altitude. Visibility was minimal to nil.

The East German and Russian radar jammers began to send their jamming signals as we neared Berlin. Our double radar receivers began to jam and the screens filled with bright static then dark screens. "Damn, there they go," yelled one of the navigators. The other navigators were operating the new secret navigation systems, which gave instantaneous positions as we approached the airfield. At that point we were relying solely on the new guidance system. Our radar was useless.

The East Germans could see that our radar was out, yet we continued our approach to the field. I'm sure they wondered when we would abort the flight or crash while attempting to land in the terrible fog without radar capability.

We approached the field along the American corridor maintaining our altitude and direction. We neared the end of the runway and could barely see the diffuse haze of the landing lights. It was necessary for the huge Globemaster to drop suddenly, like a roller coaster at the end of the runway. The runway was so short. Our gear was down and we touched the runway then accelerated the engines and took off again as if doing a touch and go exercise.

The pilot turned our plane in a big circle and continued down the British corridor and completed another touchdown and take off; I'm sure, much to the amazement of the East German ground radar observers. He repeated the same pattern in the French corridor and touched down. This time the pilots and engineer reversed the engines and we came to a sudden stop on the main runway. We taxied to the middle of the field, guided by a truck with flashing lights.

The pilots and flight engineers shut down the engines. We had overcome the radar jamming attempts by the Easterners. The flight demonstrated to the East Germans and Russians that if they continued the railroad and highway obstructions we would embarrass them with a second Berlin Airlift. (The first Allied Berlin Airlift occurred over a decade before in 1948 and lasted until the Soviets and East Germans opened their land blockade to Berlin).

We left the plane parked in the middle of the field so that all observers could see it and to demonstrate Allied determination to keep Berlin open. We crew rested and took time to visit Berlin and see the recently constructed Berlin Wall that sharply divided the city.

Two or three days later the fog lifted and the weather improved. The East Germans opened the railroads and the highways into Berlin. We boarded our Globemaster and took off for the West completing our mission.

Despite the Wall, West Berlin remained free.

* Soviet Chairman Khrushchev's political plan was to create a separate crisis over Berlin after the Soviet Union's unsuccessful Cuban Missile fiasco. He was again testing the young American, President Kennedy. This provocation resulted in an intensification of the Cold War between the East and the West.

Foggy Night to Berlin – Feb 1963

A monument to the Allied 1948 Berlin Airlift.

Berlin February 1963

World War II bombed building.

Berlin Wall February 1963

"Despite the Wall, West Berlin remained free..."

HIS FIRST AIRCRAFT COMMAND

Early spring 1963

Mildenhall is a small medieval town in Suffolk County, England dating back to prehistoric times and identified as a Roman site during the fourth century. Within the last eighty or so years its prominence is related to its history as a military air facility. Mildenhall served as an R.A.F. (Royal Air Force) base as well as an American B-17 heavy bomber base during World War ll.

It seems only yesterday that I visited the old stone officers quarters. A large stained glass memorial window allows colorful rainbows of light into the main oak stairwell and honors the brave R.A.F. (Royal Air Force) pilots and air crews who defended England against the onslaught of German bombers and fighters during the "Battle of Britain" in 1940 and the ensuing years of World War II.

I stood mutely in reverence viewing the images, an inspiring and humbling experience, perusing the glass window as the sun illuminated the names of those young, daring, brave airmen who served and of those who made the ultimate sacrifice for their country.

After the Second World War the U. S. Air Force, with only a symbolic British officer and small staff in charge, used this base as a major supply and landing base during the Cold War when the West was aligned opposing Soviet intervention throughout Eastern Europe.

We often visited Mildenhall when we ferried cargo for our military forces in England and Europe.

First Command

It was my friend's first flight as an aircraft commander. The plane was one of the 15th Air Transport Squadron. Will Brown selected a competent second lieutenant as his copilot. The navigator was another young first lieutenant. The engineer, a master sergeant was an older member of the squadron who had years of experience in the old C-124 Globemaster.

I joined the crew at our duty base at Chatereaux, France. The flight was returning to the United States. The flight from continental Europe to Mildenhall, England was part of our "milk run" in the squadron supply missions. The flight was unremarkable except for a continuing slight problem maintaining the proper amount of oil pressure in the inboard starboard engine. This problem was reported to the maintenance unit of the base upon landing at Mildenhall. I was told that this was not a rare problem on these old airplanes. "They require constant maintenance," claimed the flight engineer.

After a night of crew rest, we reported to Base Ops, had our preflight and our weather briefing for conditions over the Atlantic. The weather was reported as fine for the flight, only clouds forming about half way, moderate head winds, and no obvious foreseeable problems. "Should be a smooth flight," commented the young A/C. We were headed for the Azores.

Maintenance reported that they checked and the difficulty with the inboard engine had been serviced. They did not explain the specific maintenance performed. They signed off on the maintenance report. Our pilot and engineer reviewed the report. It seemed satisfactory. Maintaining such old aircraft was difficult, however the maintenance sections of our bases generally did a good job.

"Are you sure this engine is okay?" asked Will.

"Yes," confirmed both the maintenance officer and the chief ops officer, as we filed our flight plan.

"We've got a long way to go out over the water to Lajes (The Azores)," said Will to the operations officers.

"Don't worry," said the maintenance officer. He calmly walked out of the flight information and briefing room, dropped and mashed his smoldering cigarette stub into the sand ash tray at the door way.

Will turned to the crew and asked, "How does everything look, guys?"

The navigator volunteered, "If we have unscheduled bad weather over the Azores we're to divert to Iceland."

"We've been refueled to get us half way across the Atlantic," said the flight engineer.

"We are loaded to maximum weight capacity," said the flight loadmaster. "I think we're ready to go."

The crew truck drove us out on the tarmac and we climbed into the cargo compartment of the great airplane. The engineer, pilot and copilot stopped under the wing and starred with concern at the number three-engine before boarding the plane. "Hope they're right," muttered the flight engineer. "I was really worried on landing with such an unstable oil pressure."

"The maintenance crew said they serviced the engine and didn't really find anything wrong. They didn't run it up to top rpms (revolutions per minute)," volunteered one of the ground crew. "Guess they thought it didn't need it," he said to our flight engineer.

"We'll run it up before take off," the flight engineer calmly replied.

All engines started without problems. As usual, flames and blue smoke poured from the exhausts as the engines were individually run up. "Everything looks right," the engineer reported to the pilot, Lt. Brown.

We taxied out to the runway. They revved up the engines, this time for takeoff, released the brakes and with a lunge, we began to roll. We moved slowly down the runway. "Air speed increasing, okay?" yelled Lt. Brown over the engine noise into the chin microphone.

"Roger," responded the copilot and engineer together. The plane rapidly gained speed despite its heavy cargo and full fuel load as we reached the half way marker and then past the marker.

"Flaps set!" said the pilot."

Roger, flaps set," answered the copilot.

We were now past the abort point on the runway and the flight engineer yelled out over the engine roar, "Oh Damn, the rpms on number three are out of control. We're losing power on number three! I can't control number three's props."

The copilot starred out the starboard cockpit window. "Oh, Oh, it's a runaway prop."

"Can't stop now, can't stop now," Brown yelled at the copilot and the engineer. "Give me full power on the three engines, we are nearly airborne, gotta' get off the runway."

I looked out the same cockpit window and all I could see was a huge billow of smoke coming from the inboard starboard engine. I had no idea what was happening except that I suddenly felt terribly afraid as the plane violently shook.

The plane was lifting off the very end of the runway, barely over the direction lights, but did not seem to be gaining altitude. Every movement occurred in slow motion as the plane shuddered as in a surreal dream.

"Pull back, pull back," yelled the pilot, "get the gear up, get the gear up."

"Its pulling starboard, I can't straighten it," shouted the copilot.

Will Brown yelled to the engineer, "Feather the prop, do it now."

"It won't feather! I can't control it," the engineer screamed back to the pilot.

Will threw off his headphones and his seat straps and climbed out of the pilot's seat. "Pull it up. Keep it up," He blurted out to the copilot, who was pulling as hard as he could on the steering controls.

"We're going up," the copilot responded. "I got the gear up!"

Like a mechanical flash, Will lunged toward the engineer's control panel. He shoved the engineer to the side, grabbed the fuel control levers and shut the fuel off to engine three. He attempted to move the levers to control the prop pitch and feather the blades, but nothing happened.

The drag from the wildly spinning propeller pulled the plane out of the take off pattern to starboard where major buildings of the base were located. Will rushed back to the pilot seat and grabbed the controls of the plane and helped the copilot pull the plane back on a take off pattern away from the base.

We were only a few hundred feet airborne, yet maintaining that altitude. "May Day, May Day," he yelled into the mouth speaker mike. "We coming back, we're coming back. Clear the runway. Clear the runway," he radioed the tower. "Emergency, Emergency," the pilot repeated into the mike.

"Number three's stopped. The fuel's out. Can't tell about the prop," bellowed the engineer.

"It's still spinning," responded the copilot, "just spinning. It's still pulling us."

"We're coming about, look for the landing strip. Everybody look for the landing strip," said Will, now in a calm resolved voice.

"There it is, there, over there," blurted the copilot. He pointed to the port side of the plane.

"I see it. Now I see it. Check the gear. Is it still up?"

"Yeah, still up," answered the copilot. "I'll put it down. Gear going down."

I could feel the plane shudder and falter as the air speed changed. "Keep the engines on full power," Will turned and yelled at the flight engineer.

"Full power on all remaining engines," answered the engineer in a calmer voice.

"I think we can make it!" cried out Will, "Yeah, by damn, I think we can make it."

We gained sufficient altitude, even as heavy as we were with the crew doing all that any one could expect to recover the plane. We missed the buildings and the radio beacon tower at nearby Lakenheath Airfield. We made a complete and wide circle around the base and headed on a direct course toward the runway. It was in sight.

"Gear down, flaps set for landing. Air speed is okay," whispered the hoarse copilot into his chin microphone. He could hardly speak.

The end of the runway appeared abruptly and we settled roughly onto it. The base fire trucks and ambulance were nearby, just beyond our wing tips at runway's edge, sirens blaring above the engine noises.

"Reverse engines," the pilot called out to the copilot and flight engineer.

Number three propeller was still slowly spinning, yet barely pulling us toward the starboard side of the runway. "Keep on the runway," Will calmly said to the copilot.

"Roger, got it."

The plane rolled to a stop, just off the active runway. One of the fire truck's crew prepared to spray the dead engine. The propeller had stopped spinning as we all stared out the cockpit windows. The smoke had cleared from the engine. The firemen spoke among themselves and elected not to spray the engine with foam.

No one could speak. No one could move. We had just escaped death and we had nothing to say. The navigator, a catholic closed his eyes, tilted his head and crossed himself and mumbled something. The crew quietly ran down the checklist and shut down the remaining engines. We peered at each other and sighed. We silently climbed down the crew ladder to the ground and wandered over to an area just below the involved engine and stared up at it as if we had never seen an aircraft engine before.

Within a few minutes the base maintenance truck pulled up. The guys got out and walked slowly toward us. We stood there mute. I thought our pilot was going to slug the first maintenance person who said a word, but he didn't. He only glared at them and pointed his trembling finger toward the engine, shook his head, and we walked silently away toward the awaiting crew bus to Base Operations.

As we entered Base Ops, no one spoke to us. We got some Cokes from the drink machine and slouched down just inside the briefing room where the Ops personnel stood silent and starred at us. A grim faced major stepped from behind the briefing counter and walked over to Lt. Brown. He was the first to speak. He said nothing about the emergency landing. He only said, "I've got maintenance on the phone and they can talk to you about your plane."

Lt. Brown, clenching his teeth, looked at him and remarked, "That was the engine they worked on." He turned to us and muttered, "What do you think guys? Do you think they can fix that damn engine?"

We grimaced without answering. I suddenly realized what we had just been through. I began to feel sick. I tried to swallow but my throat was too dry. I was suddenly more scared, just knowing how close we had been to a major disaster. I excused myself and went to the bath room where I splashed my face with cold water and stared into the mirror for a couple of minutes and held tightly to the lavatory basin sides. I felt better. I came out to the Ops counter where the crew was talking to the major, the Chief Ops officer.

The Ops counter was slightly elevated so that the major was talking down to us. It was as if he was giving us orders rather than discussing our aircraft and our situation. He seemed heedlessly detached from the reality of our plight. There was a decided difference in rank and power here. He was a major and our aircraft commander was first lieutenant and he was leaning on the young lieutenant.

I reflected, this was Lt. Will Brown's first flight as an aircraft commander and all the high cards belonged to that damn major, right there in front of us.

"What do you mean four hours?" Will angrily said to the major. The major had just told Will that maintenance would have his plane's engine fixed in four hours for take off.

What I didn't realize was that because of our problem the base would have a flight maintenance delay registered against their base. It seemed he was using his rank to intimidate the young lieutenant into flying an unsafe plane.

"I don't think they can fix it in four hours," Will protested to the major. "I'm the aircraft commander, and I think we should take a crew rest while they work on the engine."

The major looked at Will's single silver lieutenant's bar on his flight jacket and said emphatically, "Lieutenant," with the emphasis on Lieutenant, "I said they could have that aircraft ready to go in four hours." He slowly turned away as to imply that the discussion was over. He had made his point. "Go talk to weather and file your new flight plan," he gruffly ordered.

Will stood immobile with an air of frustration and simmering anger. What could he say to this son-of-a-bitch, whose maintenance crew had nearly cost him and his crew their lives? He turned and gritting his teeth asked, "What can we do, Doc?"

During the discussion with the major, I realized that my life was also on the line in this confrontation. I couldn't remember ever being so distraught. I eased out from the rest of the crew toward the Ops officer, moved up to the Ops counter and quietly said to the major, "Sir this crew is not going anywhere today."

He turned with a frown of disbelief, glared at me and said, "Who in Hell says so? I've already told your flight commander to get his ass over to weather and file his flight plan." He looked at my flight jacket and saw two silver bars, a captain. He out ranked me and he couldn't believe I had just defied him and told him that this crew was not going anywhere.

"Sir," I said, "this crew is grounded!"

He now starred at me, squinted his eyes behind his glasses and a cynical smile appeared, "And on what grounds, would you say, Captain?" He smirked.

"Fear of Flying according to the book, sir," I answered.

(The Flight Regulations say that if a pilot or aircrew member, who is rated to fly, refuses to fly on a charge of "fear of flying," he must meet a court-martial board and would likely be dishonorably discharged from the service).

"What do you mean, fear of flying, Captain," he now calmly asked, shaking his head.

"I'm scared as Hell," I mumbled, "and this crew can't fly today."

He couldn't believe my response. He glared at me, again paused and took a deep breath, "And who in Hell are you to say this crew is grounded, Captain?" he yelled.

"Sir, I'm the flight surgeon for this crew and for the 1607th. I say this crew has just narrowly missed death because of poor maintenance on your god damn base," I nervously responded and glared back for a few seconds. I could feel myself tremble with anger. "This crew is not psychologically able to fly any airplane at present. They are grounded in "the interest of flying safety," I said bluntly.

The Major stammered as he looked down from the Base Ops counter. He paused, got his breath, cleared his throat, and then he calmly asked, "Captain, will you sign a medical grounding?"

"I will Major! I would rather sign the grounding papers than have to write up this whole damn conversation," I answered.

I knew I could face a court-martial for the statement about "fear of flying," but the "in interest of flying safety" is the trump card. No one may argue against the quasi-legal term without a full investigation of the whole situation by an official Flying Safety Board. This Major wanted no military investigation on his record.

"Okay, Doc, you have crew rest for twenty-four to forty-eight hours, but we should have the engine ready for your flight tomorrow," he declared. "I'll call maintenance and let them know." He stumbled through a stack of forms and handed me the grounding papers.

I filled out and signed the papers, handed the major the originals and a copy to our aircraft commander who carefully folded the papers and slipped them into his flight suit pocket, close to his heart.

With that done we went to our quarters, showered, and met for dinner at the officers club and got drunk, very drunk.

The following day we flew out of Mildenhall to the Azores and then home to the States. My friend, Lieutenant Brown accomplished his first flight, as aircraft commander. He saved his plane. He saved his crew.

"That's the engine they worked on ... Guys, do you think they can fix it?"

Royal Air Force Base, Mildenhall, England

An officer approaches wet quarters.

TDY IN PARIS, C'EST LA VIE

Easter 1963

That Easter I was not TDY in Paris but was with one of my squadrons in Chatereaux, France. On some weekends I was able to sign out to the regular assigned medical officers at the base hospital. As a flight surgeon, I could cut my own orders so I decided that an R and R (Rest and Relaxation) would be a good thing, especially with Paris so near. All I had to do was hop on the train in civilian clothes, passport in my pocket with a few francs and head up through Orleans to Paris.

"Doc," one of the bright young lieutenants from our squadron said, "if you wear those plain black Air Force shoes they'll spot you in a second as an American tourist."

"What should I wear?" I curiously asked.

"Italian shoes," he volunteered. "Yeah, Italian shoes."

"Aren't they expensive and where can I get 'em?" I asked. "Certainly not at the BX."

"Nope, you have to get them in Paris. I don't think any of the shops in Chatereaux have any. The locals would price them too high 'cause they know you are an officer and they think you can pay the price."

He added. "You may not know it, but these French like us for our money. If the base didn't have such a big French payroll De Gaulle would have run us all out years ago. They have already forgotten we chased the Germans out of France. It's all business to them."

"Did you notice the F-104s on the runway with Iron Crosses on them? A German squadron just arrived with the NATO exercise. Now the French and Germans are big friends."

"Well, I'm not buying Italian shoes just to go to Paris for a few days. Anyway those Italians make their fancy shoes too narrow for my feet."

"You'll do a lot better in Paris picking up girls with Italian shoes," he commented.

"I'm going to see the sights," I answered with a grin. "Any way, I've already treated too many of you guys who went to Paris and saw the wrong sights."

"Okay, Doc, have it your way."

The train left the Chatereaux station at 0800 on a cold Friday in March. I boarded the train dressed in the most native outfit I could assemble, a white shirt with a heavy black wool typical high neck French sweater, gray wool pants, and a tweed gray jacket. All I needed was a black beret.

The first thing the train conductor looked at as he punched my ticket were my black, plain-toed, shiny shoes. "Going to Paris, 'eh soldier?" he said in broken English.

"Mais oui," I answered in my best French. He chuckled as he handed me my punched ticket and turned back into the train car's passageway.

I was alone in the second-class compartment when the train began to jolt and move out of the station. A few miles or so toward Paris the conductor opened the compartment door and seated a family of four, two adults, and two little kids. "Bonjour," the father greeted me and then settled his family in the compartment. His wife handed him a wicker basket. It was soon apparent that my two years of high school and one year of advanced college French would not do, so we spoke in fractured French and broken English.

We were barely settled when the father opened the basket, popped the cork on a lovely bottle of red wine, broke bread as his wife sliced the cheese. He offered me a big piece of bread and cheese and a glass of the red wine just produced from the basket.

"For you," he said and we toasted "Viva la France, Viva la America!"

I then toasted, "Vive Mes. Lafayette.

He grinned, his white teeth sparkled, "Oui, Lafayette."

My lieutenant was wrong. There were some French who still loved us.

"J'ai fait l'armee quand j'etais jeune!" he boasted. (I was in the army when I was young).

"Je vois," I answered. We were all smiles.

The ride was pleasant. The family got off in Orleans and I thanked them for their hospitality. "Merci, pour le pain, le fromage et le vin," I said.

"De rien," the father answered as he packed his family off the train and waved from the platform.

In the Paris railway station I stepped off the train with my brown paper shopping bag stuffed with shorts, socks and one shirt folded about my camera. I refused to carry a suitcase. I wanted to fit in as best I could. I walked from the station glancing secretly at my crumpled Paris map looking for directions and a cheap hotel.

Near a small statue of Voltaire at a narrow intersection I spotted a little hotel. I entered the tiny foyer and walked into the small marble floored lobby, rang a bell that sat on what I thought was the registration desk. A few words of mixed French and English got me an attic room, up three flights.

I laid a few "new francs" * on the desk. She counted out the amount for a few days, gave me a slip of paper, "la note," and pushed the remainder of the francs back toward me. Pay in advance. I realized. "Merci," she said. She handed me a key on a brass pendant with the hotel's emblem embossed on the brass. The young lady pointed toward the stairs, nodded and smiled.

"Do you have bags?" she asked.

"Non, seulement ce sac en papier." I answered.

"Oh, I see!" she responded in perfect English.

The room had one single iron frame bed, one straight back chair, an empire wardrobe, a porcelain wash basin and pitcher on a small wooden table in the corner, towels and a small window that swung open and looked out over the quaint, narrow, cobblestone street. I was delighted with my find. Down the hall was the "salle de bain, les toilettes." I never found a shower and assumed after inquiring without success that the basin and pitcher would have to be my spot bath site.

* The French government devalued the currency so that the useable notes were called "New Francs."

I ventured out to the street and walked a long distance toward what I thought was the Champs Elyses, only to finally give up and hail a taxi. I kept the brass key and holder in my pocket. I wrote down the address of my hotel so that if I got lost at least I would have the address and could get a taxi back in case I lost the key.

As I climbed into the little taxi the driver started without my telling him where I wanted to go. I was confused. I wanted to go to the Eiffel Tower and the Arch of Triumph but for some reason in my best-attempted French I leaned toward the front seat and announced, "L' Arc de Triomphé, s'il vous plait."

The driver turned and with a disgusted look responded, "Dis ess de Arc de Triomphé!" and he pointed his bony finger out the window at a distant arch.

I forgot my French and answered in English, "I mean Eiffel Tower if you please!"

He shrugged his shoulders, shook his head, darted into the rushing circle traffic and turned the car about and headed for the Tower. I was glad to get out of his cab when we arrived. I paid him in new francs as best I could count and he skirted away. He did not smile.

On the top of the Tower I met two cute American girls from Texas who were spending their college year abroad in Paris. We lunched on one of the Tower landings and they invited me back to their apartment. We met several times during my visit. A day later we dined at the "Cafe de la Paix." by the Opéra Garnier. It was so expensive, we ordered only soup, salad and bread with a little red wine. One of the girls had a car so we enjoyed the terrifying traffic of Paris. I did not drive, since my license was an international one solely for use with American military or UN vehicles.

They were both delightful girls, each slender with soft auburn hair and special smiles. The cutest, Jane and I wrote for a while, but my distant assignments ended any possible long-term relationship. She invited me to go with her to one of the Spanish Islands, Minorca to meet her family who would be vacationing there. Regretfully, I was unable to go.

When I returned to the base one of our squadron's young navigators came up to me and said. "Hey, I wish I had known you were going to Paris. I have a cousin who is there for a year. She's at the Sorbonne."

"Oh," I said, "I've already met someone in Paris."

"She's cute, and I think you would like her," he insisted. "I don't have her picture, but let me write down her name and address and telephone number. When you get back up to Paris look her up," he repeated, "yeah, I know you'll like her. She's a southern girl."

Roger wrote out her name, address, and phone number in Paris, folded the paper and handed it to me. I started to put the slip of paper in my wallet then I unfolded it. I looked at the name, Jane, and address and exclaimed, "I can't believe it. This is Jane, the cute girl I'm seeing. C'est la vie!"

A few words of mixed French and English got me an attic room,"
up three flights.

"Dis ess de Arc de Triomphé."

A FRENCH TOWN AND
LINEN TABLE CLOTHS

There's nothing like a fine little restaurant with linen table cloths, napkins, polished silver, and porcelain dinnerware. That's just the kind of restaurant I enjoyed on my visits to the town of Chatereaux, near our Air Force base in France. Just a few kilometers down the rural road, through lush farm lands, small stone cottages, and occasional hedge rows was the quaint town, at least it seemed like a quaint town to me at the time, now many years ago.

A short walk from the snug little buildings in the old town was the Cathedral Saint André. Destroyed during the French Revolution, it was rebuilt in the mid nineteenth century and has served unnumbered generations of worshipers. How many baptisms and weddings and funerals has this edifice served? I wondered. With respectful awe I often visited the church. In the nineteen-sixties the services were still performed in Latin, a universal tongue that even I, though not a catholic could follow. The cathedral's ambiance always satisfied my worshiping needs.

Happily our squadron kept an old, black four door Citron for those transiting the base. We never knew who owned the car. It was simply there, keys available for anyone's use. Many days and nights it transported us about the countryside and into the town.

One of the stops in the town was the famous Jimmies that enticed our men for the night's entertainment. "If you haven't been to Jimmies, you haven't been to France," I was told. There we drank the local beer and wines, listened to small musical groups and had a darn good time. Jimmies also provided available companions for the night, not to be missed by our troops.

Yet, my favorite, spot was the little French Café on a busy corner of a narrow intersection, not too far from Jimmies. I wish I could remember the name. The checkered white and black tile floor, the lovely oak panels, and the small pastoral oil paintings carefully hung on the walls were typical of the mid-century European dining establishments.

The highlight of the evening was to slip into the bright restaurant, to be met at the door by the diminutive maitré de in black trousers, crumpled white shirt, a little bow tie, slightly tilted, and the typical warm, welcoming French smile. He would greet us with a happy, "Bon Jour Monsieur," and lead us to our favorite table by a tall window overlooking the busy side walk and narrow cobbled stone street. "C'est O.K.?" he would inquire.

"Mais oui," I answered in my marginal French. How delightful it was to sit at the table with all the amenities of the French cuisine, the white table cloths arranged with lovely settings and a small crystal vase of freshly picked white and yellow flowers, the colors depending on the season, and the busy waiter, le garçon, his white apron flying in the breeze as he delivered the first bottle of the house vin blanc or rouge.

He stands erect, twisting the cork and the slight pop entices us as he opens the slender clear bottle and pours the first sip for a taste. He smiles slightly, nods approvingly, as we properly and briskly swirl the wine sniffing as if we knew what we were doing then sipping and toasting the group. "Bon appétit."

The fine French bread and the delicious potage devoured, the main course of poisson grillé spécialité presented, then a mousse dessert ingested, ending a wondrously simple dinner.

Our bill, le note, in those days modestly priced, served and paid, we left the café, a satisfied, group of young happy soldiers.

RECIFE AND THE HOUSE OF BLUE LIGHTS

During the international power struggles of the Cold War, our government was eager to prevent the Soviets from gaining a political foothold in areas of the world critical to our national interests. We were the major contractor for the United Nations. We assumed the responsibilities of transporting troops, materiel and other logistic items for the international organization

In Africa, we supported the development of democratic governments to avoid Communist infiltration and influence. After the Congo gained its independence from Belgium we assumed the logistics responsibility of the UN's mission during the 1960s, and during the Congo's civil war with Katanga Province. Other areas of Africa were also considered vital to our national interest during the Cold War, including the West Coast of Africa.

In the nineteenth-century Liberia began as a so-called modern day country when "free blacks" from America were transported to the region. In mid-twentieth century our state department worked to establish greater communication and propaganda capability on the continent.

To maintain that degree of communication the Voice of America set up a huge broadcasting station in Liberia to send our message of freedom to all of Africa. Our job was to deliver the radio broadcasting equipment. Our Air Transport Wing of the Air Force MATS was assigned that mission. Of that Wing, the 31st and 15th ATW squadrons were selected. We picked up the Voice of America Radio equipment at the mid western site of manufacture and ferried the equipment across the Atlantic to Liberia.

Our squadron would be in areas with no American medical facilities, therefore an Air Force flight surgeon accompanied the airlift to provide medical care. The aircrews of this mission consisted of mostly young men with one major in the lead aircraft to command the other planes. I accompanied the youngest crew of "old shaky," a C-124 Globemaster. The

161

commander was a competent pilot with considerable experience for his age and rank. We had an extra navigator aboard since it was an extended flight and would be flying over unfamiliar territory.

The first leg of the trip took us to Ramey Air Force Base in Puerto Rico. We refueled without layover or crew rest. At Ramey I first saw the huge B-52 bomber. One took off beside our wing tip as we waited in the taxi lane for takeoff. It was big and the roaring thunder of its engines was deafening. The huge wings began to "flap" as the plane lumbered down the runway and became airborne. I had never seen such a sight.

From Ramey we crossed the Caribbean at altitudes of about ten thousand feet or lower. The old Globemaster was not pressurized. Oxygen masks were required by regulation at or above ten thousand feet. It was lovely to see beautiful islands, the coral, blue and green waters as we crossed the sea. We landed in Paramaribo, Surinam (previously known as Dutch Guiana).

On landing approach, barely short of the airfield runway in dense jungle, we saw the international orange markings on parts of a Globemaster that crashed months before with loss of most of the crew. It was painful flying over the remains of one of our own planes. I was told that it was a plane from our Charleston base.

After landing at the Paramaribo we were taken by vehicle into the town, a lovely old Dutch colonial village with a deflated economy and a native population left to govern themselves with only minimal training to do so.

The hotel was comfortable. We ventured a short trip into the town before dinner. After a crew rest we returned the following day to the airfield and headed for Recife, Brazil. The plane dropped down to a lower altitude so that we could see the amazing and expansive Amazon River as it approached the Brazilian coastline. I thought the Mississippi Delta was big until we flew over the Amazon. It was miles and miles of magnificent, muddy, water meshing like long, broad, fingers with the gray Atlantic Ocean.

Recife was known as the Atlantic Ocean jumping off point. This was the shortest distance between South America and Africa for the World War II Bomber Ferry Command. This unit of the Army Air Corps ferried bombers to Africa and Italy for military action against the Axis in the Mediterranean theater of war. After we landed and taxied onto our parking location we passed a series of old World War II Boeing B-17 bombers that were used by the Brazilian Air Force.

I wondered about the history of the bombers and thought each might have its own story. They tell me every plane has a story to tell and I viewed each of the "old ladies" with respect as we rolled past. They were so elegant, proudly lined up wingtip to wingtip.

What I didn't know was that our copilot, Lt. Cooley was sizing me up. I was told in Recife by one of the navigators that I recently dated his old girl friend and he was worried about my intentions. I had no intentions. For me the military was a break between two periods of poverty by choice as the medical and surgical training residencies were called at our charity hospital in Atlanta.

Before entering the military I signed a contract to return for further surgery training. I felt it was unfair to involve any other person, especially a wife in the life of a surgical intern or resident. I had difficulty understanding my friends who had taken the marriage route during early medical training. Too many of them were less than happy. Too many divorced.

After a while I was comfortable with our copilot and I reassured him that the young lady in question was a friend and lovely though she was, that was all there was to our relationship.

We were met at the airfield by an extended military automobile and driven into town to a small hotel, known as "Cora's Place." We were not allowed to wear flight suits or any military uniform in the city unless on a special assignment associated with the American Embassy or recognized American Military Attaché. We were advised not to go into the city without some local attendants and since our time was so short we chose other options. Cora's Place provided a small Volkswagen van or bus that would take us to a bar restaurant near by in the middle class neighborhood, away from the slums but not in the main city. "Why, yes, we'll take it," we all agreed.

After showers and a change to civilian clothes we headed into town. We were dropped off about dusk at a place called the "House of Blue Lights." The bus would shuttle us back to Coras.

It was an upscale bar-restaurant and what I didn't realize at the time was a "House upstairs" with "hostesses" to accommodate the gentlemen. I had never been to such a place, though the crews knew all about these establishments. The wedding rings were absent as some were bachelors for the night.

The older guys and I enjoyed our dinners with a few indescribable, but delicious drinks from the bar. We settled in comfortable lounge chairs and with only the dim blue lights shimmering and soft music playing, a number of lovely young ladies with short skirts, high heels, and low cut blouses, descended upon us like a covey of quail. "Hi boys," they softly called out. "Is there any thing you need or anything we can do for you?"

For the moment we all demurred, but after we bought and sipped a couple of more drinks, for the ladies and for ourselves, I noticed a couple of our crew were missing. The hard core crew members and I remained in our chairs or on our bar stools and watched the action as candidates left one by one. I could just imagine who I would be treating before we arrived back home.

Late in the evening we rounded up our crew and counted heads to be sure no one was missing before we headed back to Cora's Place. We assisted a couple of our guys into the little Volkswagen, waved, goodbye to our hostesses and the House of Blue Lights.

By 0600 we were showered and after Cora fed us a breakfast of scramble eggs, fried potatoes and coffee we were on our way back to the airfield. The sun rose brilliantly over the Eastern horizon welcoming a new and beautiful flying day for this first class American crew, now recovered from the House of Blue Lights. We were soon airborne out over the Atlantic as the sun climbed over the morning haze.

"Ascension is out here somewhere," said the junior navigator. He and the other navigator busily plotted on their chart and after a miscalculated sun fix the younger lieutenant commented, "I know it's about here, Charlie."

The senior navigator commented, "Lets get another fix." He pulled out his sextant to see exactly where we were.

"Good job, guys," called out Lt. Cooley to his navigators. "I can see Ascension off to the Southeast at about ten degrees and about three or four miles." The pilot was also using the directional radio beacon from Ascension for guidance.

"I knew I was right," proudly exclaimed the younger navigator to his pal. "I was just a little off. It must have been the wind direction that pulled us off a bit."

"Yeah, not bad," said the older navigator.

We flew over the tiny island and glanced at its tall radio antennas that we could clearly see with our binoculars. We continued the long leg journey across the Atlantic. "The weather looks good. We can switch on the auto pilot," said the aircraft commander to his copilot, "and alternate rests."

"Roger," said the first lieutenant from the right seat. "How do things look on the panel?" he asked the flight engineer.

"Every thing looks good, so far," replied the flight engineer. We settled down to the remainder of the long droning flight east to Africa.

"Cora's Place" – Recife, Brazil
Note the Volks Wagon vehicle.

BACK TO RECIFE

At Roberts Field, Liberia, the air was hot and stifling as we rolled to a stop by a huge, rusty, tin hanger. Several rough looking trucks appeared with a consortium of men as our giant clam doors opened to deliver the radio electronic equipment.

Our pilot descended from the plane and was met by a tall English speaking Liberian and an American sun burned diplomat in short sleeves and walking shorts. Our loadmaster spoke to the civilians. "Unload here and we will carry the equipment into town for assembly," the man from the Voice of America directed the off loading crew.

We were driven into Monrovia to a small hotel on the edge of town. Passing by local markets I was struck with the beautiful blue indigo cloth and bright colorful clothing. I am told that for ages the purple blue dyes of Liberia and Nigeria were used in the most desired fabrics in Equatorial Africa.

Once in our hotel we changed into civilian clothes and dined in a local café. We avoided the local water and asked for bottled carbonated water, "Schweppes, if you please."

"Careful of the greens," one fellow said. "Last time I was here, I suffered all the way back home."

We crew rested and the next morning returned to the aerodrome and headed west across the Atlantic. It was a smooth flight across the water. We encountered only slight western head winds. We passed over Ascension and later asked for landing instructions in Recife. We taxied by the lovely ladies, the Boeing B-17s of the Brazilian Air Force, all lined up and shiny off to our right. Our trip carried us back to Cora's Place and by evening to the House of Blue Lights.

Her mother's brother or some relative owned or at least managed the "House." I never really knew, and she approached me as my crew and I sipped the mysterious pink drinks provided by the House. I had talked to her briefly during our previous visit. "I'm not one of the girls," she boasted, I'm a manager." We sipped our drinks and she sat closer to me on the plush velvet sofa. "You are different," she whispered. "You are not like the others." Why didn't you go up stairs with the girls?" she directly asked.

I mumbled something like, "I'm just here to relax."

We talked for a while. She said she had relatives in the States and she had visited in California where her uncle owned a winery in the Napa Valley. After a few more drinks she took my hand and whispered, "Come with me. You're nice."

I had no intentions of any liaison, but after the several drinks of unknown, but strong and tasteful ingredients, my resistance failed me. I took her small, soft hand and we climbed the stone stairs to the second floor.

Down a dim hall we entered a small room, showered and she directed me to a tall worn Portuguese mahogany door and into a dark room. The balcony doors were open and a warm, wisp of air filled the room.

The moon was barely up in the night sky, yet lighted the room with a hazy, shimmering, dim, glow. She stood in a sheer white gown as the light from the balcony outlined her slender form. She moved closer to me, touched my lips, turned, slipped to the side of the room, lifted the cool crisp sheets and invited me in.

It was nearly sunrise when she nudged me. "All your men have gone," she whispered. I slipped out from the sheets, quickly dressed and she led me to the latched door down stairs. She scribbled her address and a pencil drawn line on a sheet of bright, blue stationary directing me the few blocks back to Cora's Place. With moist large brown eyes she looked up at me and with lovely English she murmured, "You will come back?"

I nodded, "Hope so."

She touched my lips and whispered, "Be safe 'till you return."

The street was empty. The street washer had just passed as I stepped onto the wet, shiny pavement bricks, and briskly walked following the little map she made for me. They were getting breakfast at Cora's as I knocked on the locked front door. A dark skinned, gray haired, woman opened the door. She smiled and with a simple hand gesture invited me in.

I showered, dressed into my flying togs, sat down to Cora's eggs, potatoes and coffee. Soon we left in the blue Chevrolet for the airfield. We taxied by the now glistening B-17s in the bright sun light and were shortly airborne north, headed home.

The crew members were quiet as we thought about Recife. I never returned.

BERMUDA TRIANGLE

Mystery or no mystery?

The SAC (Strategic Air Command) refueling unit on our base flew the KC-97, a four-engine propeller driven airplane, used to refuel the nuclear carrying B-47 jets that maintained an airborne presence around the clock.

The SAC flight surgeon was temporarily reassigned and it was our responsibility to send a flight surgeon to the unit. They maintained an underground nuclear protected command post and storage site for weapons and crews as well as the communication center.

"The SAC commander called to ask you to participate in one of their refueling missions," my NCO said. "He wants you to spend time with the crews."

"What kind and how long will we be gone?" I asked.

"The colonel says they're sending a refueling plane to Bermuda for engine maintenance and exchange and the plane will be there several days 'till the engines are serviced," the sergeant responded. "They leave tomorrow at 0600."

I arranged to leave the office and assigned one of the doctors to be in charge while I was absent. I received my clearance code identification card and headed out to the SAC site. The airman in the transport truck dropped me off at the gate. No outside vehicles were allowed inside the "fence." After I identified myself to the sentry guard and after he telephoned the command room, the locked personnel gate opened and I ventured a short distance into the underground facility.

There, I swapped my identity card for a card that could be used in the restricted areas. "Doc, we're going to refuel one of the bombers on the way to Bermuda and you'll get to see what we do out here," said the SAC commander. He proceeded to introduce me to the air crew members that I did not already know.

Our SAC unit flew an assigned area corresponding to the "Bermuda Triangle" extending from our eastern shore to Bermuda Island in the Atlantic. There was also a SAC refueling unit stationed at Bermuda. It was common to exchange planes and or maintain those planes, both stateside and on the island. Though Bermuda was a British possession we had maintained air and naval bases on the island during and since World War II.*

Shortly after O600 the air tanker rolled down the runway full of jet aircraft fuel headed for the Atlantic and our refueling mission. The KC-97 looks like a double bodied B-29 with what appears to be two fuselages pilled up vertically on each other. The design is necessary to carry so much aircraft fuel.

Well, out over the Atlantic the pilot announced, "We'll meet the B-47 shortly. We should make contact within fifty nautical miles." We were in the Bermuda Triangle, the area that mystified so many after spooky stories suggested bad omens for flight crews. One of the stories was of a missing navy squadron years ago during the Second World War that simply disappeared in the Triangle without a trace. Other planes also were reported missing in the Triangle. There were stories and myths of ancient ships mysteriously vanishing.

"Don't worry Doc, we don't believe all that stuff," volunteered the navigator. "Some folks think there is some magnetic problem out here and if that's true it explains some of the mystery stories we've heard. We think they got off course and probably ran out of fuel but no one knows why radio contact was never received from those missing planes and ships that disappeared."

The sleek B-47 bomber was right on time. Our pilot adjusted the air speed as the bomber eased up under the tail of our aircraft. Over the roar of our engines the boom operator yelled, "Doc, Come on back here and watch what we do."

The nose of the bomber nestled under the tail of our aircraft like a baby whale nosing up to its mother to nurse. I could clearly see the pilot as he aligned the refueling receptacle on his plane beneath our plane's long fuel nozzle. The fuel boom operator adjusted the boom nozzle toward the incoming plane.

Steadily the boom operator and the B-47 bomber pilot maneuvered in place and connected the fuel line. Refueling began. After a couple "break offs" or disconnections I could clearly see the B-47 pilot's gloved hand wave to the boom operator, "thumbs up" and he dropped below our plane and fully refueled, disappeared. He would remain aloft for another eight or nine hours. He would be replaced by another "atomic bomb" carrier before he headed to his home base.

We landed in Bermuda and my classmate from medical school, Navy Lieutenant Joe Tatum, the local navy doctor met our plane and scurried me off to his family house for a few days. Bermuda was a delightful and coveted assignment. We toured the island and I had an idea of what it was like to live on an isolated site in the Atlantic Ocean. Since there was no natural water the population collected rain water into cisterns storing the water under ground, in this case under the house. To save water a sign was placed in the bath room, "No Flushing after Number One." A few days later with our plane's maintenance completed, all four engines exchanged, we headed back to the States. Another successful mission for the SAC refueling squadron was accomplished.

* We received the right to maintain a military presence when President Franklin Roosevelt negotiated the "Lend-Lease" agreement with Britain. During the early part of World War II Britain faced severe food, fuel and material losses from German submarine (U-boat) attacks on their Atlantic shipping. We agreed to "loan" or "lease" the British navy our older destroyers to escort the endangered vital maritime supply convoys across the Atlantic to England.

"After boarding the KC-97 at 0600 we headed for the "Bermuda Triangle."

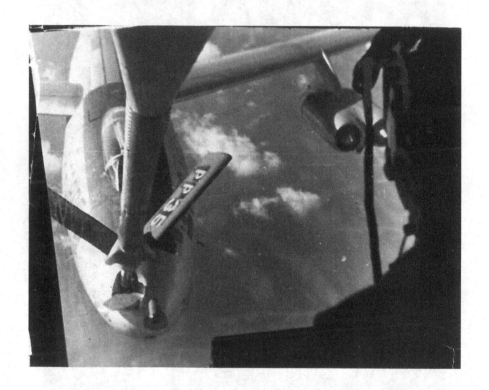

Bermuda Triangle

"The nose of the bomber nestled under the tail of our aircraft
like a baby whale nosing up to its mother to nurse."

COLONEL CRAIN IS ON THE LINE

"Colonel Crain is on the line," my office airman announced.

"I'll take it in my office."

"Yes, sir," I responded as I lifted the secured phone receiver.

"Doc, we've got a problem over here on the flight line and I'm not sure how we should handle it. Perhaps you better come over to the squadron so that I can discuss it with you.

"What kind of problem is it?" I asked.

"I'm not sure, but it requires immediate attention. We have an airman on one of the missile loading teams who thinks he can detonate one of our nuclear missiles." There was a long silent pause. "Yep, that's what he thinks."

What in the world? I thought. "I'm on my way!" I answered and hung up the phone. I grabbed my hat, told the staff sergeant to schedule any patients that came into the office for the other doctors. I would be at the 98th Squadron headquarters.

Our Air Defense Command airplanes were equipped with several missiles, one of which was a tactical air-to-air low-grade nuclear missile. Those airplanes remained on constant alert and were rotated on a regular basis. The weapon systems were loaded and unloaded, routinely, on a set time schedule so that our planes were always ready for defensive action against any would be-attacker. Those missiles were also capable of air to ground or air to sea response.

I drove through the two security gates at the squadron entrance without showing my identification. The security guards were expecting me, knew my car and had the gates opened. I arrived at the squadron headquarters and the commander met me outside the main building. "I have only a secret with a need to know security clearance, not a top secret clearance," I said to Col. Crain as we walked quickly into the headquarters. "Can you discuss these missile details with me?"

"Why, yes," he said. "This comes under the need to know part of your clearance. Shall we talk to the airman first so that you will have an idea about the potential danger of all of this?"

"Yes," I answered.

The young airman was seated in the commander's office with the operations officer and the squadron security chief. "Gentlemen, the doctor and I will talk to Airman," and he called him by name, "alone if you will excuse us," Col. Crain said.

We sat quietly in the office, the commander behind his desk and the airman and I in two chairs, side by side, facing Col. Crain. "Now tell the flight surgeon what you told your loading team leader and me."

"Yes, sir," the airman answered. He stared at me with a restrained though anxious smile. He looked to be no more that eighteen or nineteen years old, was neatly dressed, held his crumpled, billed flight line cap tightly in his folded hands. He had no other unusual mannerisms, nor evidence of being agitated or depressed. Only his inappropriate smile alerted me that all was not right with him.

He started by saying that he began to have strange feelings when he was around the nuclear missile. He said that he began to fantasize that he could make the nuclear missile go off if he wanted to. "The key lock and unlock procedures make it work, make it loaded and ready to go off," he said. "Some times I worry about those thoughts when I go to bed at night," he volunteered. He looked down at his feet then up at the ceiling and I noticed the formation of small beads of sweat on his forehead. The room was air conditioned, always too cold, I thought. It was not the temperature that caused him to sweat.

"How about the sidewinder missile? That is not a nuclear weapon. Do you ever have strange feelings about that weapon?" I asked.

"No sir," he answered. "Just, the big one. I thought that if I had all the keys I could make it go off. Sometimes I'm slow in putting my "stop" key in the key slot and wonder what would happen if I didn't put the right key in at the right time. It scares me when I get that urge," he explained.

Perhaps, he really thought he could detonate the weapon. I honestly didn't know if he could or couldn't. I knew I would have to ask Col. Crain to explain it to me. We continued our conversation for a little while. "Son, I think we better take you off the loading team until we straighten this problem out," the commander quietly said to the young airman. "You may go now."

"Yes, sir," the airman answered. He slowly stood, still squeezing his cap in his fisted hands.

Col. Crain said, "We'll notify your team leader that you will be temporarily off the loading team. We will reassign you to the administration section for now."

"Yes, sir," the airman again responded.

"That will be all," Col. Crain said. "The doctor will talk with you some more at the flight surgeon's office tomorrow. Check with the operations officer, Major Chappy, for the time." The young airman saluted and left the office. "What do you think about that young man?" the Colonel asked.

"Sir, I think he has no business around those missiles. I'm sure everyone thinks about the possibility of one going off accidentally, but I wonder how seriously they ever think about detonating one themselves," I said.

"Well, he can't detonate one by himself, but I worry about those thoughts even being present. With the "Buddy Loading Team" system, no one alone can detonate any of the weapons. The loading keys are not interchangeable and it would take several of the loaders in some major conspiracy to detonate a weapon. Even then it could not be done without the addition of manipulation of some of the electronics of the air craft," he said. "That would require the pilot to be involved."

I didn't inquire about the pilot's involvement. I didn't think that information was within my need-to-know.

The Colonel further explained how the weapon system worked. There were secrets that the loaders weren't privileged to know. A simple explosion could be achieved as with any conventional explosive, but not one with a catastrophic nuclear reaction.

The commander then walked me into the Alert Hanger where several "Birds" were on wartime stand by alert. Nuclear and conventionally armed Voodoo fighters were on constant-starting generators, ready to be airborne within three minutes. He walked me through the whole series of procedures and explained the safety features within the "Buddy System" of the weapons loading team. I felt relieved after learning the safety measures. I was surprised that the airman in question had qualified for the loading team. He was the youngest with the lowest rank on that select team.

I met several times with the young airman in my office. We talked about his personal life and it seemed he had no obvious problems. "I had above average grades in high school. Rather than be drafted into the Army I volunteered for the Air Force after high school," he said.

He was unmarried and wasn't having any girl friend trouble. He seemed like a loner with only a few friends, all air force buddies. I could find no obvious conflicts with his family who lived in a different state. He had a year and half before he was eligible for discharge. "I'm not sure I'll reenlist," he said.

I discussed his case with the base hospital commander and we sent the airman to Philadelphia Naval Hospital for a neuropsychiatry consultation. Ultimately the psychiatric department gave the man a clean bill of health that would return him to the loading team. It was my professional and personal feeling that this airman was asking for some help, though I couldn't determine the reason. Perhaps the loading team was too stressful. I didn't feel that he should return to the flight line and recommended against it. The squadron commander agreed.

The last time I saw that airman; he was doing administrative duty in the squadron office and part time in the kitchen. I made it a point to speak to him whenever I visited the squadron headquarters. I wanted him to know that he could be seen in my office whenever he needed our care. He was okay with his present position and was proud of the fact that he had been on the missile loading team, a select but a stressful job. He left the service with an honorable discharge after he served his draft commitment. He did not reenlist.

The 98th FIS Alert Hanger

IN THE BARRIER

It was a light day in the Flight Surgeons Office. While discussing the duty schedule with my staff and without warning the phone rang. "Doc, the crash truck just called, they've got a problem at the end of the runway. One of the fighters crashed into the barrier. The fire trucks are already alerted," said the base safety officer.

I grabbed my helmet and ran out the door to the Cracker Box (Ambulance). "Hurry sir," the driver yelled, "we want to beat the fire trucks." (To beat the fire trucks was always a competition even with practice exercises).

We rushed down the access road through the gates onto the active runway and toward the crash barrier. "There she is," the driver yelled, "I can see her tail up in the air."

There was a T-Bird (T-33, single engine jet) tangled in the crash barrier cables, but luckily no fire. We were almost alongside the fire truck.

"Looks like they beat us, Doc," the driver complained.

"Its okay" I yelled back. "No fire yet."

We were lucky. The fire truck nearly collided with us when my driver swerved up as close as he could get to the airplane's wing. We leaped out of the ambulance before the fire truck began the foam spray. The corpsman and I climbed upon the wing and onto a ladder the fire crew had just placed beside the fuselage.

In the cockpit was a single pilot, my good friend, Ken Upchurch. He was strapped in the seat. He had obviously hit his head. There was a large scrape across his helmet, which cracked his sun visor. He sat, dazed. We unstrapped him and pulled him out before a fire could start. "What happened?" I yelled at him.

He looked up and smiled, "Damned if I know!" He was all right.

Colonel Crain, the squadron commander, was right behind us. We got Ken out of the plane, with the help of the fire rescue men onto the ladder next to the wing.

"Don't talk to any one," the commander shouted at Ken.

"Yes, sir," mumbled Ken.

"Right," I said. We had lifted Ken out of the cockpit, now off the ladder and the step area of the wing. The landing gear had collapsed in the barrier so there were only a couple of feet to lift Ken down. By this time he was helping himself. We moved him as fast as we could to the ambulance. "Hop in the back." I blurted out to Colonel Crain. "We'll take Ken to the Hospital and check him out."

We got Ken in the back of the ambulance. "Colonel Martin (the wing commander) is really going to be upset," said Colonel Crain. We've just screwed up his base safety record."

Our fighter squadron was a tenant squadron on a Military Air Transport Base and not popular with the more subdued Air Lift Squadrons. Our hotshot pilots were frequently in trouble with the wing commander. He tried unsuccessfully to get the fighter squadron moved to another base. I was caught in the middle. I served both the fighter squadron and the air lift squadrons.

We arrived at the hospital. The medics carried Ken into the emergency room on the ambulance stretcher. "Take him to X-ray and get a skull series and a chest and full spine series," I ordered the corpsmen. "Don't let any one talk to him. Tell, even the Wing Commander that the doctors are checking him out and he can't be disturbed. No one is allowed."

Only Colonel Crain and I, with the medics attended Ken in the X-ray department. The squadron commander said to me, "We've got to keep Colonel Martin away from Ken or it will be hell to pay if he questions Ken." He paused for a moment, "I think I know what happened."

Ken looked up from the X-ray table, "I think the cowling came up as I was taking off. I tried to abort the take off," he meekly said.

Colonel Crain frowned at Ken, "Did you do a ground check or walk around?"

"Well, I thought I did," said Ken, feigning memory loss.

Crain glanced at me, "He didn't check the cowling before he took off. It must have been loose or not secured by the ground crew." He repeated, "It will be hell to pay if Colonel Martin questions Ken."

"We'll just have to hide Ken till Col. Martin cools off," I whispered. "Just tell him the docs are working with the patient and he can't be disturbed. Say Ken may have a concussion and he can't talk to any one until the medics are better informed. Then, we will decide what to do."

Colonel Martin stormed into the Emergency Room, mad as an old speckled, wet, hen. "Where is that damn pilot?" he demanded from the corpsman. "Where is that kid?"

"Sir, the flight surgeon and the other doctors are working on him right now. They think he's had a head injury, some kind of concussion. They said to check with Colonel Block," cautiously answered the young corpsman.

I knew Dr. Block would calm the wing commander down. Martin was now in Block's Hospital where the wing commander's authority was diminished. Col. Block was of equal rank. He was courteous but he didn't take any guff from any one, even the wing commander. Those on flight status rarely argued with the hospital commander who held their medical records and determined their medical ability to fly. Many of the older officers had medical waivers that could be pulled if the occasion required.

We examined and X-rayed Ken, reviewed the films, then quickly packed him away in the hospital ambulance with a couple of corpsmen en route to the Naval Hospital by the time Colonel Martin returned to the Emergency Room,

At the Bethesda Naval Hospital a neurologist and neurosurgeon were on staff. With a bang to the head and possible concussion he would have to be checked out completely by the specialists before he could return to flying status. He was temporarily grounded and safely away from the wing commander.

Colonel Crain could work out the details of the accident and reduce the cost by calling around to other fighter bases for spare parts, to repair the airplane. This would now be reduced from a major accident to a minor incident, thus appeasing the wing commander and not blotting his base's safety record.

The wing commander hurried out the hospital doors and stood on the emergency room platform and watched the dust of the departing ambulance disappear down the hospital road.

A SUSPECT

Major Perry stood at the admission desk talking to the corpsman in charge. It was unusual to see the administrative officer in the flight surgeon's office. My phone rang.

"Yes," I answered. "What is it sergeant.?"

My first sergeant was on the line and quietly announced, "Major Perry would like to talk to you in private, sir."

"Sure, send him in."

The husky, mild mannered, but serious officer slowly shut the door as he entered the office and took a seat across from my desk. Without any initial conversation, he leaned forward as if to whisper a secret. "Doc, did you know that the Air Police have been following you when you were off duty?"

"They what?" I asked.

"Yeah, it's kind of a long story. You've been a suspect in a pornographic investigation."

"In a what?" I incredulously responded.

He stammered and said, "Don't worry it's okay. You've been ruled out."

I sat quietly for a moment and wondered what he was talking about. "You mean the APs have been following me around when I'm off duty?"

The major nodded affirmatively, "Have you lent your car out to anyone?"

"Not that I can recall, except that Sgt. Brewer took my car out for a set of new tires a few weeks ago. No one as far as I know, drove my car from there. When I've been out on a trip the car's been in the base parking lot or at my house. If anyone used it, it was without my knowledge."

"Well, the police in town reported a man in a white Chevrolet coupe with Georgia license plates trying to pick up young girls to be photographed naked."

"Damn, I've got a car fitting that description."

"A couple of the girls reviewed several photographs. One was yours mixed in with a bunch of other photographs and they did not identify you as the suspect. They said he was a younger fellow. Are you sure someone else hasn't been driving your car?" the major again asked.

"Nope, no one," I answered. "How many times has someone been trying to pick up girls?"

"Several," he said. "I don't know exactly how many."

"We can check to see if any incidents occurred while I was away from the base. I'll get my flight records." I started to rise from my desk.

"We've already checked and you were not away when these occurred. You were in town."

I pushed back in my chair. "Major, I don't know what to say. The only cameras I have are a small 16-millimeter Minox that I keep in my flying suit, an Argus-C-3, and a small 8 millimeter movie camera for flying photos. Those cameras wouldn't be useful for such purposes. Whoever it is must have some sophisticated camera equipment, maybe a studio with lights and stuff."

"Well, Doc, I wouldn't worry about it, but I thought you needed to know," the major said.

"Major, I'll keep a sharp lookout for any car like mine."

The major rose from his chair. "Yeah Doc, just thought you ought to know."

COAST GUARD STATION AND A SURPRISE

During lunch at the 98th Squadron building the commander said, "Doc, as you know we lost a "101" out over the Atlantic a few months before you arrived on base with no recovery of the aircraft or crew. It just disappeared off the radar." He glanced around the room and shaking his head he added, "It's imperative we have a successful water survival exercise."

Captain Jim Madrey approached our table and sat down. Col. Crain glanced at Madrey and said, "Jim, you and the doctor will go down to the Coast Guard station to coordinate our schedule with their operations officer for the water exercise. We'll be using their boats for our crews to enter the water and our choppers for the water pick up." He then announced, "We've determined the survival exercise will be in the icy water at Lakehurst, New Jersey that simulates the winter Atlantic waters. We've got to be prepared for cold water with the new rubber survival suits."

Capt. Madrey, a tall, likable, red headed officer and I drove the few miles along the Delaware beach to the Coast Guard Station, to coordinate the exercises. We pulled into the parking lot and I noticed a white Chevrolet coupe. On further inspection I recognized a Georgia license plate. The Chevy was the same year as my car.

Upon entering the station I spoke to the Coast Guard lieutenant, "There's a white Chevrolet similar to mine in the parking lot. Whose is it?"

"Oh, that car belongs to one of the sailors," he said. "He's sitting right over there by the radar set." He was a young fellow who looked to be no more than nineteen years old. He barely noticed my presence. We didn't speak.

I curiously glanced at the sailor and thought, He's so young, he probably doesn't even shave.

We entered the lieutenant's office to plan the water exercise and I asked, "Does that sailor have any hobbies?"

"You mean the kid with the Chevy? Yeah, I think he does a bit of under water photography," he said. "He's right good, his buddies say. Why do you want to know?"

"On no reason. I just thought it's interesting that we should both have similar cars, each with Georgia license plates and stationed in Delaware."

The following day I walked into Major Perry's office and casually shut the door behind me. He gestured that I take a seat. "Any progress on your pornography investigation?" I asked.

"Not yet," he responded.

"Well Major, I think we've found your mystery white Chevy."

ICY WATER SURVIVAL EXERCISE

A scheduled number of our airmen from the 98th Squadron drove to Lakehurst Coast Guard Station, New Jersey for our cold water survival exercise. We were to use our new rubber survival suits, fondly known as "poopy suits," to be immersed in the cold waters of Lakehurst to simulate winter conditions of the Atlantic, an area designated as part of our Air Defense Zone.

We wiggled and struggled with help into our survival suits and once dressed lined up on the Coast Guard dock. The suits were bulky, unlike current tight fitting wet suits and had snug rubber cuffs and collars. During winter months when the Atlantic water temperature was near freezing the flying airmen were required to wear the suits while sitting alert in the alert hanger crew room. After being checked by the equipment sergeant we boarded a small Coast Guard cutter and headed out into the icy waters.

The plan was to be thrown or jump from the boat's stern into the water and to be dragged, attached to our parachute straps as simulated in a water parachute drop. The dragging behind the cutter simulated the effects of the chute being dragged by the force of the wind once in the water. The objective was to disengage from the parachute straps and to climb from the icy water into a small orange survival dingy that is attached to the parachute survival kit lines. After successfully boarding the dingy we were to float until our emergency helicopter dropped a basket line then remove ourselves from the dingy into the basket and be lifted to the chopper. We would remain in the chopper (in shifts) until all men were "rescued" then flown back to the land to be evaluated for the success or failure of the exercise.

Each of us entered the icy water and only a couple had trouble disengaging from the parachute straps. One, a known chronic complainer, at first unable to separate from the dragging straps, waved frantically to stop the boat as he coughed spouts of freezing water, yet received little sympathy from the amused remaining fellow airmen on the boat who tauntingly yelled, "Don't stop. Let's see how long he can survive." Of course the boat stopped and the guy received the help he needed, but he had to start all over and go back into the water 'till he got it right.

I realized how dangerous it would be to try to survive in the icy water without adequate protection when I tried during my time in the icy water without the protective gloves. It was like placing my hands on a piano key board and slamming the lid. It was so painful I could readily testify to the adequacy and success of the full survival suit components.

The exercise was declared complete and well done. We felt confident that should we have to eject over the ocean that we were prepared for that possibility and would survive. We changed back into our uniforms and headed to the nearest bar to celebrate our successful survival exercise.

98th Fighter Interceptor Squadron

Cold Water Survival Exercise, Lakehurst, N.J.

"We'll be using their boats for our crews to enter the water...
and our choppers for water pick."

Lakehurst, New Jersey

PARTY PUP

Now, a frequent visitor, since the white Chevy incident, Major Perry wandered into our office "Doc, the major would like to talk to you and Dr. Berkman if you have a minute," announced the desk corpsman.

"Sure, put him in my office while I see this patient"

"How about Dr. Berkman?" my sergeant asked. (Dr. Berkman was one of my off base bachelor housemates as well as a fellow flight surgeon).

"Let him know the major is here." Damn, I thought, what's up now?

We entered the office and the major formally addressed us, "Gentleman, my wife wants to invite you both over to our house tomorrow for dinner and a few drinks." Berkman agreed that a free meal and home cooking would be welcomed. "Oh, by the way you know my dog has a new litter of pups. These are beautiful black mixed breed puppies, part lab," added the major.

We arrived the next night and the chubby major met us at the end of the drive with drinks in both hands. "Thought you boys might like a Marguerita to start the evening." We began to sip our drinks as we headed toward the patio, joined a few other guests, and the evening dinner.

The Mexican meal was delicious, tacos and all. After several more drinks the major brought out the puppies. "What wiggly guys they are," we muttered. All seven of the pups had shiny black coats, big puppy paws, and busy, licking tongues as they assaulted us. They were everywhere on the patio. We continued playing with the pups while the major poured more drinks for us.

"Wouldn't you like to take a pup home?" he inquired. By ten o'clock we could barely see.

One of the other guests suggested that he should drive us home. "You guys can leave your car and pick it up tomorrow. It's Saturday." He drove us home. We apparently dozed in the back seat of his sedan.

Saturday morning arrived with two big headaches. I struggled out of my bed and headed for the kitchen and coffee. Is that barking I hear, I wondered? The sound came from down our basement stairs in the party room. I opened the door and headed down the stairs.

A hoarse whisper came from Berkman's room, "What happened last night?"

"I don't remember," I answered. "I think we got a dog."

"A what?"

"I hear a dog barking, I think we got a dog."

At the bottom of the stairs were little tails wagging and little black fur balls whimpering, and little puddles glimmering. I yelled back up stairs, "The major laid it on us last night."

"What do you mean?" answered my pal.

"It was those Margueritas. Oh, damn, we don't just have one dog. We've got two."

HOT SHOT PILOT

Lou was a hot shot fighter pilot and was one of my favorite guys. I flew with him in the Voodoo F-101 B more than with anyone else. We flew parts pick up trips, which did not require a certified radar observer / navigator in the plane's back seat. In the flight simulator the instructors taught me to use the radar in the 101 on low and high altitude intercepts. When the radar observers did not want to fly or had their required mission hours or there was a slot open, I was allowed to participate in the practice air intercepts. I kept my name on the ready assignment board and was called, even in the middle of the night for intercepts.

The "intercepts" were practice identifications of planes entering our (ADIZ) Air Defense Identification Zone along the East Coast from south of Washington, D.C. to above Maine, overlapping the Canadian Zone of Defense. Our planes participated with the Canadian Air Defense Command for North America. They also used the McDonnell Voodoo F-101B as part of their Air Force inventory. Our planes and equipment were interchangeable. We worked well with the Canadians as a defense team.

We usually flew with regular flight suits when flying below certain classified altitudes, but when we flew above fifty-thousand feet altitude we were required to wear the partial pressure high altitude suit. The suits were rarely if at all worn on practice intercepts.

Most of our intercepts were at the mid altitude level. Some of the flights both in the T-33 and F-101 were routine exercise training cross country flights, sometimes serving as the intruder plane into other regions of the Air Defense Command. We would serve as the radar target plane to be identified or intercepted.

These were fun flights for me. We were limited to a certain amount of diversion that we could employ as the target plane. In some of the evasive maneuvers we dropped chaff, a stream of aluminum foil to confuse the responder aircraft or to block or interfere with his radar reception. These were conventional methods of confusing the responder aircraft that originated in World War II. The Air Defense Command graded the performance of different squadrons. Our squadron always scored high on the intercepts.

One method of identification was to fly alongside the intruder and record the tail number and report it directly to ground control radar that was directing the intercept. Our squadron practice exercises were over the United States territory. We did not have intercepts over Canadian territory. We would infringe on their territory only for the real thing.

There were a few areas along our east coast where our radar had difficulty with reception in the early 1960s. These were known as "dead zones" in the system. Our squadron knew those areas and we would drop below the radar net and buzz the incoming and outgoing merchant ships along the coast. Since we were not allowed to break the sound barrier over land our squadron would perform maximum speed and other maneuvers out over the ocean. We were forbidden to produce a sonic boom over civilian populated areas.

Once our assistant operations officer, Capt. Christiansen, took me out over the Atlantic a couple of hundred miles, in a dual control F-101B and allowed me to break the sound barrier. "Take the stick," he said. "Watch the speed indicator," he yelled into the microphone.

It was exciting to watch the speed indicator approach and pass through the red marked speed of sound, some seven hundred fifty nautical miles per hour. There was a slight buffeting of the plane as we passed the sound barrier and became supersonic, then a loud boom occurred that seemed to come from behind the airplane. The sound disappeared for a second and it seemed to remain behind us as we maintained that speed beyond the sound barrier.

It was barely noticeable when we again became subsonic. The F-101 was listed as capable of 1.7 Mach speed. The commander at a squadron dinner party presented me a gold 101 pin to wear in my civilian coat lapel signifying that I had broken the sound barrier.

Early one spring afternoon my friend, Lou and I were flying along the Atlantic coast and he elected to buzz a Liberian freighter as it meandered along in the water below. Our first buzz was met with waving by the ships crew as we tweaked our wings passing close over the ship. On our second fly by Lou suddenly pulled the plane into a sharp and steep climb. The G-forces pressed me into the cockpit seat, nearly taking my breath. We drew several additional G-forces (Gravity Forces). "What was that?" I mumbled through my intercom mike.

"Gee, Doc. We were below the seagulls following that ship and I was afraid we'd suck 'em into our intakes," answered Lou.

We headed back toward the base. We neared the shore and without notice the fire warning light came on for one of the two jet engines. "We've got a warning light on," said Lou in an unexcited voice. "I'm not sure why. I know we didn't hit any of those darn birds."

A few seconds later, he came back on the intercom. "We'll have to shut that engine down and fly on the other one. If the light stays on I'll start the fire extinguisher in that engine. It should be okay. It's probably a malfunction of the light indicator."

A couple of minutes later he spoke again over the intercom, "Doc, if we have trouble and have to eject, I'll be sure you go out first. Look around and be sure the red ejection knobs are clear so you can reach them if I tell you to," he said. "I'll blow the cockpit cover then you pull your red handle knob. Soon as you feel the wind you go right out. Keep your elbows in close. You know the procedure, don't you?"

"Yeah, I know the procedure from the trainer. The handle knob looks clear," I responded. I began to think about the possibility of ejection. The fire warning light did not come back on after he shut the engine down and we flew toward the base.

Lou called the base tower to notify them of our situation and the tower transferred the call directly to the squadron commander who came on the radio.

"How much fuel do you have aboard?" the commander asked. Lou reported our available fuel on board.

"What about the warning light? Do you smell smoke in the cockpit?" asked the commander.

"Light's off and no smoke, repeat, no smoke in the cockpit," answered my pilot.

"Roger. Use up all the fuel you can and when the gauge is well below one quarter, begin your approach to the runway. On approach push the restart button. Try to restart the engine about five or ten miles out. If the warning light comes on again shut it down and try to land on one engine. We'll have the fire trucks out along the runway. Good luck."

"Roger. We understand," radioed Lou.

"Doc, I've never landed on one engine except in the simulator. I think it will be okay," said Lou through the intercom. "Just hang on and I'm sure we'll be all right." We flew around circling the base. I could clearly see the whole airfield. About a quarter of an hour later we began to make our descent to the direct glide path.

"Doc, I'm going to try to restart the engine. If you smell or see smoke back there let me know and we'll shut it down again," he calmly said. We were right on the glide path as the navigation needle pointed toward the indicated runway number. "Restarting the engine, now," said Lou. "No warning light so far." The end of the runway was in sight. We were right on line.

We touched down smoothly with only a brief high pitched skid and I felt the drag chute inflate as we jerked slightly and slowed down. Lou immediately shut down the problem engine. The fire trucks sped along the runway as we came to a slow roll and turned off the active runway to the taxiway.

Lou popped the canopy and it rose slowly letting in the fresh air from the outside. I slipped off my oxygen mask, leaned forward pressing my face against the edge of the cockpit and open canopy and took a deep breath of the cool air. The nauseating odor of the JP4 jet fuel exhaust vanished from the cockpit. How good the cold fresh air felt.

We rolled to a stop in the fighter squadron section of the field, about sixty yards from the other fighters, lined up in a row. The fire trucks and the ambulance surrounded us on the tarmac.

Lou glanced back at me through his rear mirror. He removed his oxygen mask, unbuckled his shoulder straps and with a devilish smile quietly mumbled, "Cheated death again!"

Hot Shot Pilot-F-101B on the tarmac

'We rolled to a stop in the fighter squadron section… Lou looked back
in his rear view mirror...."

98th FIS
Captain Dale "Chris" Christensen, Operations Officer

Captain Thomas "Pre" Ball, Chief Flight Surgeon

First Lieutenant Lou Shehi, Pilot 98ᵗʰ FIS

Captain "Chuck" Ewald, Navigator/Radar observer, 98th FIS

The Author (flight surgeon) testing survival "poopy" wet suit.

Captain. Jim Madrey and Lieutenant Bucholtz by the tarmac.

FRYING PAN

My NCO and I strolled down the quiet hospital hall. Holding his partly chewed and unlit cigar behind his back, he said, "Col. Block said it will be dusty and hot so be sure you have your summer clothes and gear."

"I just spoke to the squadron scheduling officer," I answered. "The 31st and the 15th Squadrons will take the first flights for the exercise. I will go with them."

"How long do you think you will be gone?" asked Brewer.

"Two weeks, maybe three at the most," I said. "Surely you and the other doctors can run the flight surgeons' office while I'm gone." Sgt. Brewer, the senior non-comissioned officer of the flight surgeons office, had accompanied the flight surgeons before on a number of airlifts away from our home base. He would not be going this time.

"Yes, sir, we can handle it. They say Texas is mighty hot this time of summer," said Brewer.

"Well, it could be worse," I said. I was not sure how.

As usual, we were delayed in our initial departure, much to the dismay of the wing commander. He was a West Point graduate and a colonel. He commanded the whole base. This command slot usually required a brigadier general. Our wing commander was passed over for promotion while all of his "West Point" classmates retired or made general. He was an excellent officer, but the other officers said his politics left something to be desired in his climb to the top. I thought he ran a darn tight ship and I respected him. I liked him. I was aware that many fine officers are passed over for political reasons, sometimes because they fail to bend the rules, sometimes because they fail, like in any other profession to kiss up to their commanders. He was like that. He was a good officer. He was not happy with any flight delays or bad marks on his base's record or any negative reflections on his career.

The four engines of the old Globemaster began their high-pitched whine, then their roar, sputtering flames and the usual blue exhaust. We taxied out, headed down the runway and were soon airborne.

"Gear up, flaps adjusted," the pilot (one of my bachelor house mates) yelled over the thunderous sound of the engines.

"Gear's up, flaps set," responded the copilot, Capt. Rozman.

"All engines on full power, oil pressures looks good," called out the flight engineer from the plane's control panel behind the pilots. We set our course for Fort Hood, Texas.

I was warned, but I never believed that a base could be so hot and so dry. I wondered where even the cactus got its water. I saw only sand, dust and heat waves rising from the ground as we settled on the runway at Fort Hood to begin our combined paratroop, infantry, and tank exercises.

"Park it over here," the ground crew signaled. "We'll unload old Shaky here."

"Old Shaky" was the name fondly given the C-124 Globemaster transport. Those planes flew until they literally shook apart. I had in my vague orders to "Participate with the Army medical units during field exercises and establish field hospitals as directed by conditions." What that really meant was a mystery to me. Such vague orders always were worked out by hit or miss communications between the military branches.

"Over here," said a burly Army master sergeant as he directed me to my assigned building. "You're Air Force, I see.".

"Yes, Sergeant, that's right."

"Your colonel says for you to come over to Building number seven. All the fly boys are over there," he said. To Building #7 I went.

Inside Building # 7, a khaki, tin, quantset hut, the officers were gathered around a long planning table. On the table was a scale model map of Fort Hood and the surrounding area used for military maneuvers. They hardly noticed my entrance.

After a few minutes a major walked over to a desk I was leaning on,"Doc, we don't have much to do at present with the Army's field hospital. We'll give you a Jeep and driver. You can get about the base to check on the other airmen."

An army private saluted me as I climbed into the dusty jeep. He was my driver, not over eighteen, lean, clean shaved, with a G.I. haircut, and a single stripe on his khaki sleeve, signifying he was a private first class. "Where to, sir?" he asked.

"I don't know soldier, just a ride around the base so I can figure out where I'm going."

"It's mighty big, sir." We drove and drove and it was mighty big, mighty dusty, mighty dry, and it was mighty hot.

We returned from our tour of the base, dodged big trucks, heavy armored vehicles, and tanks along the rough gravel road, often having to pull off and allow the huge vehicles to pass. "We can't argue with those big tanks," the soldier yelled as the noisy vehicles rumbled by, grinding the gravel road.

We parked the Jeep in the shadeless area by the command post. "Private, you take the rest of the day off. I can handle this Jeep."

"I can't sir, my job is driving," he heartily protested.

"Thank you Private, I just don't see any need for you to stand out in this damn hot sun waiting for me to decide to take a ride. See you in a day or so." I said. "We'll call the motor pool when we need someone."

He mumbled something about gas, then responded, "Yes sir, an order is an order." He handed me the keys, saluted and he was gone.

After hanging around the command hut, I decided to go out to the tank range and watch the initial maneuvers. I climbed into the Jeep, squeezed under the steering wheel, started the engine, shifted the floor gears, and drove out the winding road toward the range.

A few miles out, in what seemed the middle of the desert, the engine began to sputter and the Jeep came to a gradual, chugging halt. I looked about the dashboard and I couldn't believe I was out of gas on the loneliest, hottest road in Texas. I slipped out of the seat, walked to the back of the Jeep and picked up the five-gallon gas can from the rear of the Jeep. I shook it gingerly. Empty! I couldn't believe it. The soldier tried to tell me but I had shushed him off before he could warn me of the low gas level.

Surely someone would come along. I climbed upon and sat on the Jeep's hood and decided to simply wait and thought surely someone would stop and help. I didn't smoke so I entertained myself by humming, Deep in the Heart of Texas.

Thirty minutes later two GIs roared up with dust flying, slammed on brakes, skidded in the gravel, and inquired, "You got a problem, Captain?" as they attempted to hide their laughter. "You're Air Force, aren't you, sir?"

How dumb, I thought. Out of gas in an Army Jeep. They will have a good time with this back at the barracks. "You got any gas in that Jerry can?" I asked.

"Yes, sir, we do," they responded and took the can off the rear of their Jeep and poured its contents into my gas tank. "Better get to the gas station. This isn't much," a fellow with two stripes on his sleeve said, "just a couple of gallons."

I arrived at a long line of huge, grimy Army vehicles at the fueling station. By the time I got through the haze of gas and diesel exhaust fumes to the gas pump I was chugging on my own fumes.

"Fill 'er up," I told the husky army sergeant in his oil-stained overalls. He did without spilling a single drop.

"Some in your Jerry can?" he asked. He gazed at the vehicle. "What are you doing driving a Jeep, sir?" he asked as he noticed my Air Force fatigues. "Where's your driver?"

"Don't have a driver," I said.

"But, you're an officer," he replied as he filled my Jerry can with gasoline. "Officers don't drive Jeeps."

I didn't answer. I just looked at him and shook my head, all the while thinking about those two young soldiers who had given me their gas. They were probably still laughing.

"You got your gas card, sir?" he asked.

"What gas card?" I answered.

"Sir, You gotta' have a gas card to get gas."

"I've already got the gas," I said. He took his fatigue cap off, rubbed his sweaty brow with an oily rag,

"What are we gonna' do about it, how can I charge you? We'll be short on charging," he said.

"Sergeant, just charge it to that big damn tank in line behind me. The Army will never know the difference."

"Yes, sir." He ran his grimy rag back over his forehead and waved me on, out of the gas line and motioned for the big tank to move forward.

A few days later the joint military exercises began. I was invited to go above the Army tanks and infantry in a helicopter that looked like one of those two man bubble choppers in "Mash."

"You like to fly this thing?" the Army pilot asked.

"Never flown one before," I answered over the roar of the helicopter engine and swishing propellers.

"Its just the opposite to a regular plane, push instead of pull," he said. "I'll show you."

"The only thing I've flown myself, so far is one of the Aero's Piper Cubs, a tail dragger, and that was with a real pilot." I answered.

"Just try it," he said.

"Okay, here we go."

After I made a couple of uncontrolled, teeth shattering landings and near misses of some base structures, he decided that this flight surgeon was better in the operating room than in the cockpit. He was generous. "Not bad," he said. We flew chopping along back to the base-landing pad.

The following day one of the sergeants found me out on the firing range in my Jeep and exclaimed, "Hey, Captain, the Colonel wants to see you."

At Building #7, Col. Jones asked, "Doc, what in the Hell are you doing driving an Army Jeep around without a driver?"

"Col. Jones, It was just too hot to make that young private sit around waiting for me to decide when and where I wanted to ride, so I gave him the day off."

"Do you know that the Army thinks officers must have drivers. Seems to suite their egos," he said.

"Okay, sir." I handed him the keys.

"Call the motor pool and tell them to come get their damn Jeep," he shouted across the room to the senior staff sergeant.

From across the drab conference room, "Doc, there's a call for you from your hospital commander," said the staff sergeant.

On the other end of the line came a clear, bass voice, "How do you like Killeen, Texas and Fort Hood?"

"Sir, not much," I answered. "It's hot, like a frying pan."

"You want out of there?" again came a commanding voice from the phone.

"Yes, sir," I answered. "That would be good."

"Anywhere?" came the voice.

"Yes, sir, most any where!" I answered.

"Okay, we have a special mission that can pick you up in Dallas at 0600 tomorrow at Love Field. You'll be gone a long time. Can you get up to Dallas tonight?"

"I'll try," I said.

"Be there," he firmly said. "Get civilian transport or what ever way possible. Check with Col. Jones and see what they can do for you. Sgt. Brewer will send a "TWIX" to you with the orders. It's urgent. We need a flight surgeon along for this mission."

After a pause, "Do you have some cash? You may need it to get there."

"I've enough."

"Good, just keep a record and any receipts 'till you get back. You'll be getting TDY pay and reimbursed for your expenses on transportation."

"Yes, I'll check with the Army and see if they have anything special going to Dallas."

I asked the sergeant in our command post about transportation to Dallas.

He answered, "There are only a couple of commercial buses that leave the base at night, nothing military," said the sergeant. He had overheard the conversation and was already dialing information to get a commercial schedule. He spoke to someone on the phone and quickly hung up the phone. "The lady at the transportation center said they had one bus to Dallas tonight. I think you can make it."

There was one lonely pickup bus stop near us at Fort Hood after sun down. The night was dark. We stood under the single, flickering, bare, light bulb, besides the squeaking, swinging, faded, Grey Hound Bus Stop sign outside an old closed down wooden Army building. Soldiers and civilians of all descriptions waited around puffing cigarettes, sitting on boxes or suitcases, leaning against the peeling, gray, splintered wall of the building. I was the lone officer in this dusty crowd waiting for the one lone bus to Dallas.

"It ain't a direct ride," said one civilian fellow in old overalls and a crumpled western hat pulled down over his eyes.

"You mean it isn't an express," said another fellow.

"Yep, sometimes there ain't enough seats and you get left behind," chimed in the first guy.

Rank and orders meant nothing that night. It was dark with only an early waning moon, hiding behind high, floating, clouds and with that single 60-watt, dirt covered bulb, we all looked alike, just gray shadows with our boxes and duffel bags, some going home on leave and some just leaving.

"Where do we get tickets?" I asked one of the soldiers.

"Heck, you just pay the driver, no tickets," a corporal answered.

Two headlights barely pierced the night's haze as the motor coach rolled to a squeaking halt, crunching the gravel beneath its wheels. The coach seemed to settle to the ground as the front door slowly opened.

"All aboard," the driver shouted as he peered through his thick, steel rimmed glasses at the waiting bunch, his bus driver hat perched on the back of his thinning gray head, and a tooth pick between his front teeth.

We all passed under the glow of the dim light and squeezed through the door of the big Grey Hound.

"Only a couple of seats left," he muttered, now eager to pack us all in. "All the way to the back, boys," he gruffly yelled. "Ready fares. Don't have much change tonight."

The fellow in the overalls and crumpled hat moved onto the bus steps, eased up to the drivers spot, fumbled in his pockets, found a couple of dollar bills and dropped a hand full of change on the floor. The driver leaned out of his seat and frowned at the guy. "Hell, boy, don't worry about it. I'll get it later. Com'on in and find a seat, that is if 'en you can."

With payment accomplished, our band of strangers moved down the dark, narrow, aisle, dodging bags, suitcases, vegetable sacks, and Army duffels protruding from the overhead racks. This must really be the local milk run, I thought.

There seemed to be no more seats until a G.I. yelled, "Come on back here buddy. We can fit one more."

Seven of us filled the five spaces at the very back of the bus. Our heads pressed against the back window. The interior light glowed dimly. Then, it was out as the bus began to move forward and the jostling for room and the confusion diminished.

It was not long before our first stop, Waco. More sleepy eyed passengers filtered onto the bus. No one got off. Some were standing in the aisle hanging on to the overhead hand straps. As we started off again, I could hear the irregular snoring all around me. These guys were worn out. We were, weaving and bobbing, one head on my shoulder, and mine on the next fellow's as we rhythmically rolled on toward big Dallas.

Streaks of light in the gray sky shown outside the hazy windows of the bus as we pulled into the Dallas bus station. A neon sign with the letters "a," both absent from "Dallas" added little light.

I stumbled over my big khaki travel bag as I clamored down the Greyhound steps, relieved to be in the fresh, cool night air, out of the stuffy inside of the crowded, smelly, bus. On one side of my B-4 bag I usually kept heavy clothes for Arctic duty and on the other, light clothes for the tropics. This time I only had hot weather clothes. I had no idea which I would need. I could not be told my destination. At least, I thought, I was out of the frying pan at Fort Hood, which I thought, must be the Hell Hole of the Army.

Now, to get a taxi to Love Field; I worried, not many taxis at 4 a.m.. Most of my traveling companions were in the terminal changing buses or stretching out on the hard, oak benches in the pale, fluorescent-lighted waiting room of the station. I was alone on the platform.

In the stillness of the quiet, early morning I heard a hoarse, scratchy, voice behind me, "Want a taxi soldier?"

"Right," I said, "to Love Field."

The driver emerged from the shadows, took a big puff of his cigarette, exhaled into the morning darkness and flipped the smoldering butt on to the concrete platform, stamped it with his boot shod foot, coughed, and mumbled, "Yeah, son, I'll get you there."

Inside the cab I stretched out on the soft, cheap, fake leather back seat. I couldn't straighten my legs. I had been cramped on that bus seat for four or five hours without moving.

There was a special loading area at civilian Love Field for military planes. We wandered around until the taxi meter told me we had looked enough. I got out, paid and thanked the driver and walked across the pavement until I found a security officer to whom I identified myself.

I had what we called "TELE" or "TWIX," brownish, flimsy copies of rather vague military orders, which simply named me and listed my serial number among several other airmen and informally described our destination by saying, "squadron so forth will proceed to such and such destination as directed," with no real destination listed. I had no idea where I was going, but the paper convinced the civilian security guard that I was for real, perhaps lost, but obviously no threat to the nation. He allowed me to walk out on the tarmac to a huge silver Globemaster standing in the dim glow of a red rising sun over Texas.

I wiped my dry eyes, licked my parched lips, rubbed my hand along my scruffy beard and approached the giant bird dragging my bag behind.

"Hi, Doc," yelled the loadmaster from the ramp of open forward clam jaws of the great silver flying monster. He stepped off the loading ramp as the huge clam shell doors began to close. "We're all loaded, but couldn't take off. The A/C said we had to have a flight surgeon with us on this mission. We're waiting for you."

"Why me?" I yelled back.

"Your colonel said you were on temporary duty nearest to Dallas.

"Where are we going?" I yelled.

"Can't tell you. You gotta' get closer," he shouted.

I threw my bag up through the narrow hatch door way into the belly of the plane. I climbed the crew ladder into the immense cargo compartment and asked, "Now, where in hell are we going, Sergeant?"

He adjusted his flight cap, grinned slightly and I could see his white teeth as he involuntarily smiled and squinted toward me, and quietly answered, "Captain says, Viet Nam!"

I recalled the old cliche, "From the frying pan into the fire," this time worse than Fort Hood.

"... a huge silver Globemaster, standing in the
glow of a red, rising sun over Texas."

FAR EAST – PACIFIC SHUTTLE

We left Dallas en route to the Pacific by way of the West Coast to Hickham Field in Hawaii. There we crew rested and visited the town to see the hula-hula girls at the open-air restaurants and bars in swanky, down town, Honolulu.

Our evening was going well until we pulled one of the young lieutenants off the bandstand. He decided to show the Hawaiian drummer how to "really play the drums." After a few more drinks we were all invited to leave. "I've been thrown out of better places," the lieutenant yelled as we assisted him out to the sidewalk to a taxi and back to Hickham.

How eerie I felt sleeping in the creepy, old wooden barracks where our Army Air Corps men were during the attack on Pearl Harbor and Hickham in 1941. I felt the ghostly presence of those who had been there on that Sunday in December.

On leaving Hickham Air Field, our pilot flew low over the coast so we could see Pearl Harbor from the air. It was chilling to see the Naval base with the American ships all docked, just as the Japanese attackers had seen it on that infamous day.

Our next stop was Wake Island, a small island or atoll in the middle of the Pacific. I was amazed that our navigators could find such a tiny speck of land out there in the vast ocean. Wake Island was one of the first islands taken by the Japanese forces in World War II. Our small Marine and Navy garrison put up a gallant fight to defend the island. Two thousand miles away our Navy commanders felt that the island was indefensible. They were not willing to reinforce the garrison and endanger the already diminished American Naval fleet that had suffered such severe loses, at Pearl Harbor.

They wrote the island off while the small number of defenders valiantly repulsed wave after wave of invading Japanese landing forces, all the while awaiting American reinforcements that never came. The Japanese put to death many of the defenders and civilian engineers and contract workers that they found on the island after its final surrender.

After we landed, a local demolition officer, a fellow I knew at our home base met our plane. His job was to be available, should any transient plane crash or have an accident involving a conventional fire or explosion while carrying nuclear weapons. Those potential incidents were labeled, Broken Arrows.

That's all he did. He was sunburned from his stay on the island. He hurried out in the summer sun to meet us in his khaki shorts, sandals, and ragged straw hat. During my short stay he accompanied me all over the tiny island. We explored caves that the occupying Japanese forces had dug when they prepared to defend the island. Our military forces bypassed Wake during the war and recovered the island after the Japanese surrender in 1945.

My friend and I snorkeled in the lagoons of Wake and explored the remains of a partly sunken, rusty, Japanese freighter that was sent and "beached" during the war to bring food to the starving Japanese garrison.

Our next stop was Guam followed by a landing in the tail of a Pacific typhoon at Clark Air Force Base in the Philippines. I thought I had been in bad weather before, but nothing to match the end of our flight into the Philippines. "Old Shaky," our plane, earned its reputation for toughness and durability on that leg of our mission. I don't believe many other planes could have withstood the battering we received that day. I recall the pilot securely strapped in his seat yelling, "Doc, just hang on tight. Ol' Shaky can make it. We've been here before."

Our destination, an airfield outside Saigon, Viet Nam was reached after our grueling and exhausting flying experience. We taxied down the runway; I opened the top hatch and climbed out on the top of the airplane, out into the humid, sweltering heat, just to look around.

A minute or so later the flight engineer grabbed me by the pants legs and jerked me back into the plane. "Damn, Doc," he said, "don't you know there are Viet Cong snipers out there off the runway just looking for someone stupid enough to pop their head out of the plane?" He was right. I was stunned and hadn't really given it a thought. At that young age, we all felt invincible.

We later flew to Bangkok and our planes ran a shuttle between Saigon and Bangkok. What I didn't realize till later was that our squadrons and some CIA planes were also running shuttles into Cambodia while we helped set up radar stations that controlled the air war over Indochina. I couldn't read the signs. I didn't know the difference. It had never dawned on me that we might not be in or over Viet Nam. I thought Cambodia was off limits.

After our shuttles were completed, the task force of airlift planes returned to the United States. We approached the West Coast and our pilot flew directly toward San Francisco Bay then veered south to the designated military air corridor to enter the continental United States. We flew by the lighted Golden Gate Bridge, glowing in the dark night. It was a welcome sight, twinkling tiny lights on the bridge and auto lights rushing along as their drivers moved, unaware of the returning air craft and the impending and escalating conflict brewing in the Far East. I wondered how many American military men and women in past wars had experienced that feeling of finally arriving safely home.

"WAR HELL, THIS IS WHERE THE WAR IS."

After fourteen hours on the road I arrived at Atlanta's Grady Hospital in the dark of night. While unloading my car I tried to figure out where my quarters would be in the hospital when a friend, Will Hansom, appeared on the loading dock.

He yelled down from the landing, "Where have you been? The professor has been trying to find you. Your contract started over a week ago. He's mad as Hell."

I looked up at him standing on the dock and answered, "Hell, I've been to War."

"War, this is where the war is." He blurted out. "Don't you remember this is where the real war is, here at the Gradys?"

Will was right. I had forgotten. I had grown up in Atlanta. I knew the city. I was familiar with the Gradys. I had driven the ambulance before I started medical school and during that time I worked in the hospital at various jobs. I had interned and done a year of general surgery at the Gradys before my military duty.

Earlier that morning I walked out of the military hospital and met one of my corpsmen in the drive way. I had worked with him for nearly two years, "Where are you going now, Doc?" he asked.

"Home," I answered. "Just home."

I returned to Atlanta. I returned to Grady. I was home.

POST SCRIPT

In July 1963 I returned to an orthopaedic surgery residency at Atlanta's Grady Hospital and continued reserve military involvement as the flight surgeon at Dobbins AFB for the 445th Air Transport Squadron of the US Air Force Reserve and the Georgia Air National Guard for three subsequent years.

On the first day of duty at Dobbins Air Force Base the medical clinic's senior sergeant advised, "You need to go and meet the commanding general."

Upon entering the general's office I was greeted by the commander. "Have a seat Doc." The general picked up a manila folder with my military records and perused them as I sat quietly. He looked up from the chart, removed his reading glasses and said, "I know you. You used to ride your bike to my store. I remember you as a kid. I know your family." He paused, "You were my neighbor."

I was truly home.

The general was a bomber pilot in Europe during the Second World War and after the war continued his service with the Air Force Reserve unit in Georgia. He was in business in my neighborhood.

REFLECTIONS

Thanks to the many special friends from the
Ranch House, the Lake House and the Medical Service,
all fine Airmen, Officers, and Staff.

Richard Berkman
Ralph Briggs
Bill Brown
K. C. Cloyd
Chuck Ewald
Billy Graham
Bob Prochko
Norman Weiner
Jerry Epstein aka. Lance
Larry Gilford
Stan Lasiter
Peter Townsend
Bernard Bruner
Ed Kafel
And
Our wonderful office secretaries,
"Flo" Camac and Ruby Honeycutt

FLIGHT SURGEONS OFFICE
Dover Air Force Base, Delaware
Staff
1961 – 1962 – 1963

Block, Herbert - (M.D.) Col. Flight Surgeon - Hospital Commander

Ball, Thomas P. - (M.D.) Capt. Chief Flight Surgeon (1961-1962)
Berkman, Richard - (M.D.) Capt. Flight Surgeon
Gilfert, Larry - (M.D.) Capt. Flight Surgeon
Laster, Stan - (M.D.) Capt. Flight Surgeon
Townsend, Peter - (M.D.) Capt. Flight Surgeon
Watts, Jerald L. - (M.D.) Capt. Flight Surgeon
Bruner, Bernard - Master. Sgt.(NCO in Charge)
Kafel, Ed - Staff Sgt. Airman Medic Corpsman

Camac, "Flo" - Civilian Staff Secretary
Honeycutt, Ruby - Civilian Staff Secretary

Braden, Ed G. - Airman Medic Corpsman
Cottrell, David - Airman Medic Corpsman
Donnelley, William - Airman Medic Corpsman
Humphries, Tom - Airman Medic Corpsman
McCord, Clyde - Airman Medic Corpsman
Oberman, "Obie" Airman Medic Corpsman
Plas, Joe - Airman Medic Corpsman
Thyne, Ed - Airman Medic Corpsman

These were all good men and women.
I was proud to work with each of them.

Chronological History

Cuban Missile Crisis – Official Record of Events
October 19, 1962 – October 29, 1962
(Information edited from various sources on the internet, 2014)

Tuesday, October 16, 1962. Intelligence preliminary report of Soviet missiles deployed in Cuba was revealed and resulted in increased U.S. aerial surveillance of the missile deployment. U-2s and F-101Rs were used for the increased surveillance.

Characteristics of missile sites indicate two distinct types of instillations: Medium range ballistic missiles capable of carrying nuclear warheads to a range greater than 1000 kilometers.

Additional sites, not yet completed appear designed for intermediate missiles of greater than twice the range of medium range missiles.

Offensive rather than defensive missiles represented explicit threat to peace and the security of all the Americas. (Russians claimed only defensive weapons were deployed).

Thursday, October 18. False statements from Soviet Foreign Minister Andre Gromyko concerning the type and purpose of Russian missile deployment in Cuba.

Friday, October 19. The British are notified about the offensive missiles in Cuba and our concern.

Saturday, October 20. As a necessary precaution President John F. Kennedy ordered, reinforcement of our base at Guantanamo, evacuation of dependents and additional military units to be on standby alert basis.

Monday, October 22. President Kennedy addressed the nation by radio and television, announced the activity in Cuba and his communication with Chairman Khrushchev to halt and eliminate this clandestine, reckless and provocative threat to world peace. The president ordered a quarantine of ships entering and leaving Cuba. By political negotiation, combined with a secret agreement of the United States to remove certain nuclear missiles from Turkey, resulted in a conciliatory agreement with Soviet Chairman Khrushchev.

Monday, October 29, 1962. The Cuban missile crisis ended. Soviet ships headed to Cuba were turned back and the nuclear missiles were subsequently dismantled and removed from Cuban soil.

The serious Soviet and American crisis had drawn to an end. Both Khrushchev and Kennedy set up a telephone "Hot Line" of communication to avoid future missteps in international confrontations that would threaten the security and peace of each of the super powers.

Unofficial record of Events

(This information is edited from personal on site experience.)

Saturday evening October 20, 1962. 31st Squadron, Officers Promotion Party: Announcement of Airlift at the Party.

Sunday, October 21, A.M. To Base Operations. 31st Squadron crews airlifted to Charleston, SC.

Monday, October 22, A.M., Replace 15th Squadron crews and fly Globemasters with Marines and supplies and arms to Cuba. Assist Evacuation of dependents from Guantanamo to U.S. on flight line.
Assigned quarters at Guantanamo. Squadrons continue Airlift to reinforce Guantanamo.
Listened to President John F. Kennedy's speech to the nation on veranda at Leeward Point, Guantanamo Naval Base Officers Club. Episode with sentry and "password."

Tuesday, October 23. Monitor Air traffic and witness C135 Air Crash. Attempt unsuccessful rescue with other navy personnel.

Wednesday, October 24. Assist Washington Air Force Air Crash Investigators.

Thursday, October 25, Fly back to U.S. / Pick up 101st Airborne (Ft. Campbell, Kentucky). We await invasion instructions in Florida Air Base on the tarmac. Several "stand downs" or official delays are ordered by the president while we anticipate an airborne invasion. The invasion of Cuba is canceled. The 101st Airborne troops are flown back to their bases.

Sunday, October 29, The Cuban Missile Crisis is considered ended.

MCDONNELL VOODOO F-101 B

Standard Inventory of the
98TH Fighter Interceptor Squadron
Air Defense Command

Specifications:
Crew: 2 = Pilot, Radar Observer / Navigator
Length: 67 ft.
Wing Span: 39 ft. plus.
Weight: Empty-28,495 lbs.
Loaded-45,665 lbs.

Engines: Two Pratt & Whitney jet engines with after burners
P & W J57-P55 engines
Fuel: 2053 gallons, 2953 with wing fuel tanks
Armament: 4 – Falcon – Air-to-air missiles, fuselage weapons bay
2 GAR - 1 (AIM – 4 A) Semi-active radar homing missiles
2 GAR - 2 (AIM –4 D) Infrared guided missiles
Late Models had:
2 MB - 1 (AIR 2 Genie Nuclear rockets)

"Project Kitty Car" in 1961 upgraded weapons on F-101 B.
Four Hundred F-101 Bs were manufactured and shared with the Canadian
Air Defense.

Training Dual controlled planes were designated TF-101 B.

Photo intelligence aircraft were designated F-101 R.

The Voodoo, despite its technical difficulties was one of the most underrated airplanes in the Air Force inventory. It guarded the United States and Canada. The plane served in the Air Defense Commands of the U.S. and Canada during the most dangerous periods of the Cold War. The reconnaissance version of the F-101, along with the famous U-2 spy plane identified (the F-101 R at low level) the Soviet missiles in Cuba during the 1962 Cuban Missile Crisis.

DOUGLAS C-124 GLOBEMASTER II

A major transport airplane of the 1607th Air Transport Wing
Military Transport Service

Specifications:
Crew: 6 – Pilot, Copilot, Navigator, Flight engineer, Loadmaster
(sometimes two navigators & two engineers)
Length: 130 ft.
Wingspan: 174 ft. 1 in.
Height: 48 feet 4 in.
Wing area: 2,510 ft. sq.
Empty weight: 100,000 lbs.
Loaded weight: 195,000 lbs.
Max. takeoff weight: 216,000 lbs.
Power-plant: 4x Pratt & Whitney R-4360 "Wasp Major" radial engines,
3,800 hp.

Max speed: 320 mph.
Range: 2,175 nautical miles
Service: ceiling: 34,000 ft.

The Douglas C-124 Globemaster ll, named "Old Shaky," was a heavy-lift
transport built by the Douglas Aircraft Company.
The C-124 served as the primary heavy-lift transport for the United States
Air Force Military Air Transport Service (MATS) during the 1950s and
early 1960s until the C-141 Starlifter entered service. The C-124's design
featured two large clamshell doors and a hydraulic-ramp in the nose as
well as a cargo elevator under the aft fuselage.

As a cargo hauler, the C-124 could carry tanks, guns, trucks, and other heavy equipment or 200 fully equipped troops on its double decks. It could carry 127 litter patients and their attendants.

The C-124 first flew on 27 November 1949 and was delivered to the military in May 1950.

It performed world wide support while in the service and later was used by Air Force Reserve units. Transfers to the Air Force Reserve units were completed by 1970.

MATS was the primary operator until it was reorganized as MAC, Military Airlift Command in 1966.

The last C-124 was retired in September 1974 completing over 24 years of distinguished service.

Research for C-124 and C-133B: Wikipedia, the free encyclopedia

DOUGLAS C-133B CARGOMASTER

A major transport airplane of the 1607th Air Transport Wing
Military Air Transport Service

Specifications:
Crew: 6 – (Pilot, Copilot, Navigator, Flight engineer, Loadmaster
(sometimes two navigators & two loadmasters)
Length: 157 ft. 6 in. (48m.)
Wingspan: 179 ft. 8 in. (54.8m.)
Height: 48 ft. 3 in. (14.7m.)
Wing Area: 2673 ft. sq. (248.34m. sq.)

Empty weight: 109,417 lbs. (49,631 kg.)
Loaded weight: 275,000 lbs. (125,000 kg.)
Max. takeoff weight: 286,000 lb. (130,000 kg.)
Power plant: 4 x Pratt & Whitney T34-P-9W turboprops,
7,500 shp. (5,586 kW) each.
Cargo deck: 86 ft. 10 in. (26.47 m.)

Performance: Max. speed: 312 kn (359 mph, 578 km/h)
Cruise speed: 280 kn (322 mph. 519 km/h)
Range: 3,560 nautical miles / hour with 52,000 lb (23,587 kg)
Payload: 4,097 lbs., 6,590 km.)
Service: ceiling: 32,300 ft. (9,800 m.)
Crew: six or seven (two pilots, one or two navigators, two flight engineers,
one loadmaster)

The Douglas C-133 B Cargomaster had its first flight 23 April 1956 and
was delivered to the USAF in August 1957 (MATS). It was the only

turboprop strategic air lifter. It came out of production after the Lockheed C-130, a shorter or tactical airlifter. The C-133 was capable of transporting intercontinental missiles. The C-133 remained in service until replaced by the Lockheed C-5A.

Fifty C-133s were constructed for military airlift. Ten were lost before it ceased operation. Nine were lost in crashes and one on the ground to fire. Six of those losses were Dover 1607 ATW MATS airplanes.

During the author's service at 1607 ATW, a C-133 # 57-1611 was lost on 27 May 1962 in the Atlantic. Portions of the plane's debris floated to the ocean surface and were picked up by a German commercial freighter and brought to Dover, AFB for examination by the USAF Accident Board members.

Several C-133s were lost to configuration problems or stall problems, taking off to altitude or on landing approach. One was lost while refueling, one disintegrated in flight due to hidden structural cracks and one was lost to propeller problem (stuck in fixed position) due to electrical in propeller control or propeller electrical power circuits.

BOEING KC-97 STRATOTANKER

The Major Airplane of the 11th SAC Refueling
Squadron, 499th Air Refueling Wing
Dover, AFB, Delaware
1961- ...

Specifications:
Crew; 6 (Tanker) – Pilot, Copilot, Navigator, Flight engineer, Radio operator, Boom operator)
Capacity: 9,000 gallons (34,000L) jet fuel
(KC-97 Troop carrier version: 96 troops or 69 stretchers or modified tanker equipment)
Length: 117 ft. 5 in (33.7 m)
Wingspan: 141 ft 3 in (43.1 m)
Height: 38 ft. 3 in (11.7 m)
Wing area: 1,734 ft² (161.1 m²)
Empty weight: 82,500 lb (37,410 kg)
Loaded weight: 120,000 lb (54,420 kg) (Tanker-153,000 lbs.)
Useful load: 37,500 lb (17,010 kg)
Max. takeoff weight: 175,000 lb (79,370 kg)
(Piston engines / propeller driven) Power plant: 4 × Pratt & Whitney R-4360B Wasp Major radial engines, 3,500 hp (2,610 kW) 28-cylinders each
2X J47-GE turbojets (5790 lbf. each

Performance
Maximum speed: 400 mph (644 km/h)
Cruise speed: 230 mph, (370 km/h)
Range: 4,300 mi, 3,700 km

Ferry range: 5,000 nautical miles (5,760 mi, 9,270 km)

Service ceiling: 30,000 ft

Wing loading: 69.2 lb/ft² (337.8 kg/m²)

Power/mass: 0.117 hp/lb (192 W/kg)

The Boeing KC-97 was developed 1950 and 816 planes were built...

The KC-97 was phased out in favor of the KC-135

Primarily served to refuel the Boeing B-47

The KC-97 was phased out for the KC-135 (jet aeroplane).

Air plane References: Google / Wikipedia / Air Force Museum Information Service

SWEDISH SAAB J-29 - TUNNAN

Standard inventory plane of the UN Forces in Congo
1961 - 1964?

Specifications:
Crew: one (Pilot)
Length: 11.0 meters (36 ft. - 1 inch)
Wing Span: 10.23 meters (33 ft. - 7 inches)
Weight: Empty-4.845 Kg (10,680 lbs.)
Loaded:...
Power Plant:
Engine: 1 x Svenengiska Flymotor RM 2B - Turbo Jets
Max. Speed: 1,100 Km/hr. (660 mph.)
Range: 1,100 Km. (685 miles)
Armament: 4 x 20 mm cannons
75 mm Air Rockets
Rb 24 - air to air missiles
5.8 anti-armor Rocket
(Internal cannons, unguided missiles)

SAAB J-29 was the first Swedish jet to fight in combat
In 1961 Five J-29B planes were in Congo for ONUC
(F 22 Wing of the Swedish Air Force)
Later four more J-29Bs and 7 more J-29Cs added for the Photo
Reconnaissance.
The J-29s attacked ground targets. None were lost to ground fire.

Note: The Rebel Katanga forces used a few French Fouga Magisters (CM-170S),
likely piloted by European mercenaries.
Weight: 4,740 lbs. with a speed of 424 mph. (715 Kl/hr.)